Living in Tuscany
Vivre en Toscane

Living in Tuscany
Vivre en Toscane

Barbara & René Stoeltie

EDITED BY · HERAUSGEGEBEN VON · SOUS LA DIRECTION DE

Angelika Taschen

KÖLN LONDON LOS ANGELES MADRID PARIS TOKYO

CONTENTS

INHALT

SOMMAIRE

VILLA VILLORESI

Cristina Villoresi

Sesto Fiorentino

The infectious laughter of Cristina Villoresi rings through the "galleria" with Egyptian-style frescoes that leads to the salons and bedrooms making up the almost endless labyrinth of her magnificent ancestral home. One wonders if the echo of her voice reminds guests at the Villa Villoresi of the ancient legend that Gemma Donati, wife of Dante, took refuge in this house during the poet's exile in the early 14th century. The Villoresi family is justly proud of the villa near Florence, which began as a 12th-century fortress, was converted into a pleasure palace during the Renaissance and finally became a country hotel some thirty years ago. Proceeding from the armoury – now a restaurant – by way of the "limonaia" orangerie, and the dining room decorated in the early 19th century with popular scenes by Bartolomeo Pinelli, you arrive at what is billed as the longest loggia in Tuscany and a series of very elegant bedrooms adorned with antique-style frescoes. And in the evening, while the intoxicating scents of roses, lemon blossom and wild oranges waft through the open French windows, the mistress of the house sets the table and proves yet again that the culinary arts of Tuscany know no equal.

LEFT: *family photos on an 18th-century desk.* ABOVE: *detail of a fresco in one of the first-floor bedrooms.*

LINKS: *Familienfotos auf einem Sekretär aus dem 18. Jahrhundert.* OBEN: *ein Fresken-detail in einem der Schlafzimmer in der ersten Etage.*

A GAUCHE: *des photos de famille sur un secrétaire à abattant 18ᵉ.* CI-DESSUS: *détail d'un décor a fresco dans une des chambres du premier étage.*

Das ansteckende dunkle Lachen von Cristina Villoresi hallt durch die mit ägyptisierenden Fresken verzierte »galleria«, die Zugang zu einen verwirrenden Labyrinth von Salons und Räumen gewährt. Und man fragt sich unwillkürlich, ob das Echo ihrer Stimme wohl die Geister der Vergangenheit weckt. In einer der Legenden um die Villa Villoresi heißt es, dass Gemma Donati, die Frau von Dante, sich Anfang des 14. Jahrhunderts, während des Exils ihres Mannes, hierhin flüchtete. Die Familie Villoresi ist stolz auf ihren Familiensitz bei Florenz. Als Burg im 12. Jahrhundert errichtet, wurde er in der Renaissance zu einem Lustpalast umgebaut und schließlich vor gut dreißig Jahren in ein Landhotel verwandelt. Geht man vorbei an der ehemaligen Waffenkammer, die heute ein Restaurant ist, an der »limonaia«, der Orangerie, und am Esszimmer, das im frühen 19. Jahrhundert von Bartolomeo Pinelli ausgemalt wurde, erreicht man schließlich die Loggia – angeblich die längste der Toskana – und etliche elegante Schlafzimmer mit Fresken in antikisierendem Stil. Und am Abend, wenn der betörende Duft der Rosen durch die Verandatüren hereinweht, deckt die Hausherrin die Tische und beweist stets aufs Neue, dass die kulinarischen Genüsse der Toskana ihresgleichen suchen.

Half-moon window and balcony overlooking the inner courtyard.

Das halbkreisförmige Fenster und der Balkon bieten einen Blick in den Innenhof.

Une fenêtre en demi-lune et un balcon donnent directement sur la cour intérieure.

Le rire sonore et contagieux de Cristina Villoresi retentit dans la « galleria » ornée de fresques à l'égyptienne qui mène vers les salons et les chambres. Ceux-ci constituent le labyrinthe quasi interminable de sa magnifique demeure ancestrale près de Sienne, et on se demande si l'écho de sa voix rappelle aux hôtes de la Villa Villoresi la très vieille légende qui veut que, au début du 14e siècle, Gemma Donati – la femme de Dante – se soit réfugiée dans cette maison pendant l'exil du poète. La famille Villoresi se montre fière de cette forteresse du 12e siècle, transformée en maison de plaisance pendant la Renaissance et devenue un relais de campagne il y a plus de trente ans. De la Salle d'armes, aujourd'hui restaurant, en passant par la « limonaia», l'orangerie, et par la salle à manger décorée au début du 19e siècle de scènes populaires par Bartolomeo Pinelli, on atteint la loggia dite « la plus longue de Toscane», ainsi qu'un ensemble de chambres à coucher élégantes, ornées de fresques à l'antique. Et le soir, quand le parfum enivrant des roses, des citronniers et des orangers sauvages entre par les portes-fenêtres grandes ouvertes, la maîtresse de maison dresse les tables et prouve – invariablement – que l'art culinaire de sa terre natale est à nul autre pareil.

The "galleria" was formerly the coach entrance. The Egyptian-style frescoes by the painter Luzzi date from 1829.

Früher diente die »galleria« als Kutschen-zufahrt. Die Fresken im ägyptisierenden Stil schuf der Maler Luzzi im Jahr 1829.

Jadis, la galleria servait d'entrée cochère. Les fresques à l'égyptienne ont été réalisées en 1829 par le peintre Luzzi.

ABOVE: *In the Villoresi dining room the walls are painted with scenes from traditional folklore. The celebrated Roman artist Bartolomeo Pinelli (1781–1835) – who created these charming vignettes – was a frequent guest of the family.*

RIGHT: *a corner of the dining room. The richly decorated looking-glass dates from the mid–18th century.*

FACING PAGE: *A charming scene: small dogs in period costume, begging.*

OBEN: *Im Esszimmer der Villoresis zieren volkstümliche Motive die Wände. Der Schöpfer dieser charmanten Szenen, der bekannte Künstler Bartolomeo Pinelli (1781–1835) aus Rom, war häufig zu Gast bei der Familie.*

RECHTS: *eine Ecke im Esszimmer. Der reich verzierte Spiegel stammt aus der Mitte des 18. Jahrhunderts.*

RECHTE SEITE: *Ein charmantes Motiv: kleine Hunde in historischen Kostümen machen Männchen.*

CI-DESSUS: *Dans la salle à manger des Villoresi, les murs sont ornés de scènes charmantes inspirées par le folklore populaire. Leur auteur, le célèbre artiste romain Bartolomeo Pinelli (1781–1835) était souvent l'hôte de la famille.*

A DROITE: *un coin de la salle à manger. Le miroir richement décoré date du milieu du 18ᵉ siècle.*

PAGE DE DROITE: *Une scène délicieuse: des petits chiens en costume d'époque font le beau.*

LEFT: *In one of the main bedrooms the walls are covered with "trompe l'œil" pastoral scenes. Birdcages and statues inspired by antiquity stand against a backdrop of the Tuscan landscape.*
FACING PAGE: *Siesta time – and a warm breath of air from outside lifts a corner of the diaphanous curtain.*

LINKS: *In einem der Zimmer der Hausherrin sind die Wände mit Hirtenmotiven in »Trompe-l'œil«-Manier bemalt. Vogelvolieren und antikisierende Statuen stehen vor einer toskanischen Land-schaft.*
RECHTE SEITE: *Es ist Zeit für die Siesta, während eine leichte Brise die Vorhänge sanft bewegt …*

A GAUCHE: *sur les murs d'une des chambres maîtresses, des compositions pastorales en trompe-l'œil. Des volières et des statues à l'antique s'y détachent sur un fond de paysage toscan.*
PAGE DE DROITE: *C'est l'heure de la sieste et le souffle tiède de la brise soulève les voilages diaphanes …*

Lemons straight from the "limonaia" behind the villa, succulent tomatoes and juicy melons ready for putting up with cinnamon, rosemary and cloves.

Köstliche »pomodori«, saftige Melonen und frisch geerntete Zitronen aus der »limonaia« hinter der Villa – die Früchte werden eingemacht und mit Zimt, Rosmarin und Gewürznelken aromatisiert!

Les « pomodori » succulents, les melons juteux et les citrons cueillis dans la « limonaia », seront mis en bocaux et parfumés à la cannelle, au romarin et aux clous de girofle!

SALVIA ALLA BUTTERA

As a starter, Cristina Villoresi generally serves her famous "salvia alla buttera" (stuffed sage leaves).

Mix flour (100 g) and water in a large earthenware bowl until liquid; the batter should be thin enough to run easily down a wooden spoon. Take another tablespoon of flour and two tablespoons of water and blend with a dozen anchovy fillets into a smooth paste. Wash and dry a bunch of sage leaves, then spread each leaf with the anchovy paste and cover with a second leaf, sandwich-style. Lay out the "sandwiches" on a dish. Heat the oil to boiling point in a frying pan, dunk the stuffed sage leaves in the batter and drop them into the oil one by one. Remove with a skimmer when fried golden. Serve immediately with a glass of chilled dry white wine.

Als Vorspeise serviert Cristina Villoresi gerne ihre berühmten »salvia alla buttera«, gefüllte, frittierte Salbeiblätter.

Vermischen Sie in einer Schüssel 100 Gramm Mehl mit so viel Wasser, bis ein geschmeidiger, nicht zu dicker Frittierteig entsteht. Er sollte leicht von einem Holzlöffel abtropfen. Verkneten Sie dann einen Esslöffel Mehl mit zwei Esslöffeln Wasser und einem Dutzend Anchovisfilets zu einer gleichmäßigen glatten Paste. Dann eine Hand voll Salbeiblätter waschen und abtrocknen. Streichen Sie die Anchovispaste auf die einzelnen Salbeiblätter und legen Sie jeweils ein zweites Salbeiblatt darüber. Verteilen Sie die »Sandwiches« auf einer Platte. Erhitzen Sie das Erdnussöl in einer Pfanne bis zum Siedepunkt. Dann werden die gefüllten Salbeiblätter in den Teig getaucht und in heißem Öl frittiert, bis sie leicht gebräunt sind. Mit einem Schaumlöffel aus der Pfanne heben und sofort servieren, am besten mit einem eisgekühlten trockenen Weißwein.

En apéritif, Cristina Villoresi sert, de préférence, ses célèbres « salvia alla buttera », les feuilles de sauge farcies.

Mélangez 100 grammes de farine et de l'eau fraîche dans une terrine en faïence et essayez d'obtenir une pâte à frire homogène pas trop épaisse; elle doit couler facilement le long d'une cuiller en bois. Mélangez aussi une cuiller à soupe de farine, deux cuillers d'eau et une dizaine de filets d'anchois afin d'obtenir une pâte fine et lisse. Lavez et séchez les feuilles de sauge, tartinez chaque feuille de pâte d'anchois et couvrez avec la deuxième feuille. Posez les « sandwichs » sur un plat. Plongez les feuilles de sauge farcies dans la pâte à frire et faites-les frire dans l'huile portée à ébullition. Retirez avec une écumoire quand elles sont légèrement dorées. Servez-les immédiatement accompagnées de préférence d'un verre de vin blanc sec bien frappé.

UN RITIRO FRA LE COLLINE

Colli fiorentini

From behind its thick stone walls, this elegant villa in the Florentine hills exudes an air of untroubled peacefulness. It was built in the 16th century by a wealthy Florentine family as a summer pavilion, and is indeed a perfect place to escape from the oppressive summer heat of the city. Bought at the beginning of the 20th century by the forefathers of the current owner, it was carefully restored to its original state in the sixties. The pale ochre of the stuccoed exterior, untouched since then, the multitude of family mementoes inside and the filtered sunlight, which seems to stop, almost from habitual deference, at door and window, add to the serene if old-fashioned atmosphere, making this a true sanctuary from the rigours of day-to-day living. The loggia has been the summer drawing room from time immemorial. The stunning view of the "limonaia", the green landscape and the vestiges of a nymphæum may have something to do with this, along with the omnipresent sunshine, which makes this hidden corner of Tuscany a real paradise.

LEFT: *Stone steps leading up to the portico of the villa.*
ABOVE: *still life of stones.*

LINKS: *Eine Steintreppe führt zum Eingangsportal der Villa.*
OBEN: *ein kleines Stillleben aus Kieselsteinen.*

A GAUCHE: *Un escalier en pierre mène vers le portique de la villa.*
CI-DESSUS: *une petite nature morte de galets.*

Mit ihren dicken Steinmauern strahlt die auf einem Hügel bei Florenz gelegene elegante Villa eine angenehme Ruhe aus. Im 16. Jahrhundert wurde sie als Sommersitz einer reichen Florentiner Familie errichtet und ist bis heute ein idealer Platz, um der drückenden Schwüle der Stadt zu entkommen. Anfang des 20. Jahrhunderts von den Vorfahren der heutigen Besitzerin erworben, wurde das Steingebäude in den Sechzigerjahren originalgetreu restauriert. Der helle ockerfarbene Stucco, der seitdem unverändert erhalten blieb, die zahlreichen Familienerbstücke und das Sonnenlicht, das nur gedämpft durch die Türen und Fenster dringt, tragen zu der freundlich-nostalgischen Atmosphäre bei. Hierher kann man sich zurückziehen vor den Anfechtungen des täglichen Lebens. Immer schon diente die Loggia im Sommer als Wohnraum. Das mag damit zu tun haben, dass sich von hier eine atemberaubende Aussicht bietet: auf die »limonaia«, die Orangerie, auf die zartgrünen Hügel und die Überreste eines ehemaligen Nymphäums. Und auch die allgegenwärtige Sonne trägt dazu bei, diesen verborgenen Winkel der Toskana in ein wahres Paradies zu verwandeln.

Située sur une colline près de Florence et ceinte d'épais murs de pierre, cette villa élégante rayonne de sérénité. Elle fut construite au 16e siècle par une riche famille florentine qui en fit son pavillon d'été, et de nos jours encore, on ne peut rêver de meilleur endroit pour échapper à la chaleur oppressante de la ville. Acquise par les ancêtres de la propriétaire actuelle au début du 20e siècle, la demeure a été méticuleusement restaurée durant les années 1960. Le stuc ocre pâle des murs resté intact depuis, les nombreux souvenirs de famille et la lumière du soleil tamisée qui filtre par les portes et les fenêtres, tout cela contribue à créer une ambiance paisible et surannée, faisant de ce lieu la retraite idéale contre les rigueurs de la vie quotidienne. Depuis toujours, la loggia fait office de salon en été; la vue époustouflante qu'elle offre sur la «limonaia», sur le paysage verdoyant et sur les vestiges d'un nymphée y sont sans doute pour quelque chose, tout comme le soleil omniprésent, qui fait de cet endroit bien caché, un vrai coin de paradis.

LEFT: *In the ochre drawing room, the earth tones create an atmosphere of warmth.*
BELOW: *The knocker on the front door is shaped like a lion's head; an arched niche in the garden.*

LINKS: *Die Ocker- und Erdtöne lassen diesen Raum gemütlich wirken.*
UNTEN: *Der Türklopfer an der Eingangstür hat die Form eines Löwenkopfes; eine kleine Rundbogennische im Garten.*

A GAUCHE: *Dans le salon, les ocres et les couleurs de terre forment un ensemble chaleureux.*
CI-DESSUS: *Le heurtoir de la porte d'entrée a la forme d'une tête de lion; une petite niche arquée dans le jardin.*

FACING PAGE: *In Tuscany, the burning sunshine is a redoubtable enemy, to be thwarted with closed shutters and tiled floors providing shade and coolness.*

LINKE SEITE: *In der Toskana wird die pralle Sonne nicht geschätzt. Fensterläden, Terrakottafliesen und Halbschatten sorgen für kühle Räume.*

PAGE DE GAUCHE: *En Toscane, le soleil brûlant n'est pas un ami: les volets fermés et les dalles en terre cuite apportent la pénombre et la fraîcheur tant désirées.*

LEFT: *In the principal bedroom, the wrought-iron curves of the bedstead stand out against the painted wall panelling.*
FACING PAGE: *The kitchen, which is on the first floor, still has its original large linen cupboard, built-in larder and Thirties' wooden sink stand.*

LINKS: *Im Schlafzimmer der Hausherrin heben sich die schmiedeeisernen Arabesken des Betts von der gemalten Vertäfelung der Wände ab.*
RECHTE SEITE: *In der Küche in der ersten Etage befinden sich noch der Wäscheschrank, ein eingebauter Vorratsschrank und die Spüle aus den Dreißigerjahren.*

A GAUCHE: *Dans la chambre maîtresse, les arabesques d'un lit en fer forgé se détachent sur les murs décorés de faux lambris.*
PAGE DE DROITE: *La cuisine, située à l'étage, a gardé sa grande lingère, son garde-manger encastré et son meuble évier des années 1930.*

RIGHT: *The room has regained its original 17th-century colours, Louis Seize wing chair and footrest.*

RECHTS: *In diesem Zimmer wurde die originale Farbgebung des 17. Jahrhunderts wiederhergestellt. Auch der Ohrensessel und die Fußbank im Louis-Seize-Stil stammen aus dieser Zeit.*

A DROITE: *La chambre a retrouvé ses couleurs 17e d'origine, son fauteuil à oreilles et son repose-pied de style Louis Seize.*

ROBERTO BUDINI GATTAI

Impruneta

To begin with, it was only a modest winegrower's house eaten away by time and the weather. Architect Roberto Budini Gattai freely admits he bought it on an impulse because it had something beyond price: a view across the whole of Florence and the surrounding countryside. Budini Gattai never tires of asserting that a resolutely contemporary architecture does not exclude the application of traditional techniques, and his creations strike a balance between the pure lines of today and the colours, structures and patinas of the past. In converting the old structure, he added a swimming pool in the best Californian taste, but apart from this homage to David Hockney, he did not fail to cover the walls with a pink "stucco antico", crown the roof with earthenware vases planted with agaves and equip the window frames with traditional shutters. Inside, one is lulled by an ambience of permanent siesta: the white walls, solitary deckchair and sofa covered in a thinly striped cotton fabric supply a perfect complement to the filtered rays of the sun and discreet murmur of fountains outside the closed shutters.

LEFT: *sunshine filtering through the shutters casts diagonal shadows along the red stucco of the façade.*
ABOVE: *a decorative aperture in the door of a wardrobe.*

LINKS: *Die Schatten der Fensterläden zeichnen sich auf dem rötlichen Stucco der Fassade ab.*
OBEN: *Ein dekorativ ausgesägtes Motiv ziert einen Wandschrank.*

A GAUCHE: *A travers les jalousies, le soleil dessine des ombres diagonales sur le stuc rougeâtre de la façade.*
CI-DESSUS: *Un découpage décoratif orne un placard.*

Zu Anfang gab es nur ein bescheidenes Weinbauern-Haus, an dem schon der Zahn der Zeit seine Spuren hinterlassen hatte. Der Architekt Roberto Budini Gattai gibt offen zu, das Gebäude spontan gekauft zu haben, und zwar wegen des herrlichen Ausblicks auf Florenz und die ländliche Umgebung. Er betont gerne, dass eine bewusst moderne Architektur und alte Arbeitstechniken einander nicht ausschließen. So zeichnen sich Budini Gattais Entwürfe oft durch die perfekte Synthese zwischen den klaren Konturen des 20. Jahrhunderts und althergebrachten Farben, Strukturen und Patina aus. Beim Umbau des maroden Gebäudes ließ er einen kalifornisch anmutenden Swimmingpool à la David Hockney anlegen, und gemäß seiner Überzeugung überzog er die Mauern trotzdem mit dem rosafarbenem »stucco antico« der Toskana. Agaven in glasierten Keramiktöpfen bekrönen das Dach, und an den hohen Türen ergänzte der Hausherr traditionelle Fensterläden. Im Inneren des Hauses laden die weißen Wände, der einsame Liegestuhl und eine Couch, die mit fein gestreifter Baumwolle bezogen ist, zu ausgiebiger Siesta ein. Durch die Fensterläden dringt gedämpftes Sonnenlicht herein, während in der Ferne diskret das Wasser in den Brunnen plätschert.

Forty degrees in the shade, and the pool offers the only refuge from the heat.

Vierzig Grad im Schatten! Der Hausherr sucht Zuflucht im kühlen Pool.

Quarante degrés à l'ombre! Roberto cherche refuge dans l'eau fraîche de la piscine.

Au début ce n'était qu'un modeste pavillon de vigneron rongé par le temps et par les éléments, et l'architecte Roberto Budini Gattai avoue volontiers qu'il l'acheta sur un coup de tête parce qu'il lui offrait le luxe inestimable d'une vue panoramique sur Florence et la campagne environnante. Budini Gattai ne se lasse pas de proclamer qu'une architecture résolument contemporaine n'exclut pas l'application de techniques anciennes, et ses créations se distinguent souvent par l'harmonie qui règne entre les formes épurées d'aujourd'hui et les couleurs, les structures et les patines d'hier. En transformant le pavillon vétuste, il l'a doté d'une piscine dans le plus pur goût californien, mais, à côté de cet hommage à David Hockney, il n'oublia pas de couvrir les murs d'un « stucco antico » rosâtre, de couronner le toit de vases en faïence ornés d'agaves et d'équiper les portes-fenêtres de volets à jalousies traditionnels. A l'intérieur règne une ambiance de sieste permanente, et les murs blancs, le transat solitaire et le canapé revêtu d'une cotonnade à fines rayures complètent à merveille les rayons de soleil filtrés et le murmure discret des jets d'eau derrière les volets fermés.

The house, pool and terrace are a remarkable architectural ensemble of geometrical design and linear purity.

Haus, Pool und Terrasse bilden optisch eine Einheit mit klaren Linien und geometrischen Formen.

La maison, la piscine et la terrasse forment un ensemble architectural aux formes géométriques et aux lignes pures.

A turquoise pool, ochre-red façade and green shutters against a blue sky: Budini Gattai is a worshipper of bright colours.

Der türkisfarbene Pool, die ockerrote Fassade und grüne Fensterläden vor einem azurblauen Himmel: Budini Gattai liebt die Farbenvielfalt.

Piscine turquoise, façade ocre rouge et volets verts sur fond d'azur: Budini Gattai adore la couleur.

FACING PAGE: *One wall of the drawing room, painted jade green, is entirely made of cupboards. The star-shaped apertures provide ventilation.*

ABOVE: *A venerable, deformed olive branch on the terrace acts as contemporary sculpture.*

RIGHT: *In the bedroom, a Forties' vase and a piece of broken marble combine to make a simple but sophisticated still life.*

LINKE SEITE: *Hinter der jadegrünen Wand im Salon verbergen sich Wandschränke. Die ausgesägten Sterne dienen der Belüftung.*

OBEN: *Der gewundene Ast eines alten Olivenbaums auf der Terrasse wirkt wie eine moderne Skulptur.*

RECHTS: *Im Schlafzimmer bilden eine Keramikvase aus den Vierzigerjahren und eine Marmorscherbe ein elegantes Arrangement.*

PAGE DE GAUCHE: *Un mur du salon, peint en vert jade, est entièrement composé de placards. Le découpage en forme d'étoile se charge de l'aération.*

CI-DESSUS: *Sur la terrasse, une très vieille branche d'olivier tordue joue les sculptures contemporaines.*

A DROITE: *Dans la chambre à coucher, un vase en faïence des années 1940 et un fragment de marbre créent une nature morte sobre et raffinée.*

LEFT: *In the bedroom, the pale wood used for the floorboards, hanging cupboards and sloping ceiling is in perfect harmony with the pinkish ochre of the walls.*

LINKS: *Im Schlafzimmer ist das helle Holz der Bodenplanken, der Schränke und der Dachschräge fein auf das Rosa der Wände abgestimmt.*

A GAUCHE: *Dans la chambre à coucher, le bois blond du plancher, des placards et du toit en pente s'harmonise à merveille avec l'ocre rosé des murs.*

RIGHT: *By noon, the shutters are closed and Roberto Budini Gattai, like everyone else in Italy, is hidden away from the "sol leone".*
FACING PAGE: *in the entrance hall, a broom and a terracotta pot packed with oleander.*

RECHTS: *Mittagszeit, die Fensterläden sind geschlossen, und wie alle Italiener meidet der Hausherr die Sonne.*

RECHTE SEITE: *ein Besen und ein Terrakottatopf mit Oleander im Eingangsbereich.*

A DROITE: *Midi a sonné, les volets sont fermés, et comme tout le monde en Italie Roberto Budini Gattai se protège du soleil.*
PAGE DE DROITE: *Dans l'entrée, on découvre un balai et un pot en terre cuite où se serrent des branches de laurier-rose.*

VILLA DI TIZZANO

Elisabetta Pandolfini

Chianti

It's hard to imagine the Villa di Tizzano without its owner Elisabetta Pandolfini. It is the painter's eye and sculptor's hands of the remarkable Elisabetta that have transformed the interiors of this big, beautiful patrician house in one of the loveliest parts of the Chianti region. To visit Elisabetta is to fall under the spell of her engaging personality – especially in the great rooms where her own paintings and sculptures live in perfect harmony with the works of other artists, furniture that breathes history, and sofas, bouquets and decorative objects whose shapes and colours are endlessly interesting and original. The Villa di Tizzano once belonged to the Talleyrand family and was bought by the Pandolfinis in the 19th century. Living here, Elisabetta has chosen to turn her back on the world and focus her attention on the people she loves. It is hard to describe the unique beauty of her flower-filled garden with its centuries-old trees, or the broad terrace with its Medici urns and breathtaking view. From her attic studio, which is in some sort her ivory tower, she contemplates the landscape of Chianti and, far away, the steeples of her native Florence. The view would be inspiring enough for any mortal, but for a gifted artist it is nothing short of stupendous.

In one of the ground-floor rooms, the graceful outline of an 18th-century chair stands out against the curtains.

In einem der Räume im Erdgeschoss zeichnet ein Stuhl aus dem 18. Jahrhundert ein graziles Schattenspiel auf die Vorhänge.

Dans un des salons du rez-de-chaussée, la silhouette gracieuse d'un siège 18ᵉ se détache en ombre chinoise sur les rideaux opaques.

Es fällt schwer, sich die Villa di Tizzano ohne ihre Besitzerin Elisabetta Pandolfini vorzustellen – denn sie war es, die dem stattlichen Patrizierhaus in einer der malerischsten Gegenden des Chianti mit den Augen einer Malerin und talentierten Bildhauerhänden den letzten Schliff gab. Wer Elisabetta besucht, verfällt unweigerlich der sehr persönlichen Austrahlung ihres Hauses. In den geräumigen Salons stehen ihre Gemälde und Skulpturen Seite an Seite mit den Werken von Künstlerkollegen. Die Möbel und dekorativen Objekte überraschen mal durch ihre Form, mal durch ihre Farbe. Die Villa di Tizzano gehörte einst den Talleyrands und wurde im 19. Jahrhundert von der Familie Pandolfini erworben. Die Besitzerin lebt zurückgezogen und sucht Kontakt nur zu den wenigen Menschen, die ihr nahe stehen. Es ist gar nicht leicht, die ganz besondere Stimmung des Gartens in Worte zu fassen, mit seinen Blumen und den jahrhundertealten Bäumen. Die Aussicht von der großen Terrasse mit den Medici-Vasen gehört zu den Dingen, die Elisabetta immer wieder aufs Neue begeistern. Von ihrem »Elfenbeinturm«, dem Atelier unter dem Dach, blickt sie über das Chianti bis zu ihrer entfernten Geburtsstadt Florenz – die perfekte Inspiration für neue Werke.

Il est difficile d'imaginer la Villa di Tizzano sans sa propriétaire Elisabetta Pandolfini, car c'est l'œil de peintre de la remarquable Elisabetta et ses mains de sculpteur qui ont transformé les intérieurs de cette belle et vaste demeure patricienne située dans une des régions les plus pittoresques du Chianti. Rendre visite à Elisabetta, c'est tomber sous le charme de sa personnalité attachante et s'imprégner de l'image de ces grand salons où ses propres tableaux et sculptures côtoient harmonieusement les œuvres d'autres artistes, le mobilier chargé d'histoire et des bouquets, des canapés et des objets décoratifs qui surprennent tantôt par leur forme, tantôt par leur couleur. La Villa di Tizzano – elle appartenait jadis aux Talleyrand et fut achetée au 19ᵉ siècle par les comtes Pandolfini – ressemble à sa propriétaire car celle-ci a, comme sa maison, choisi de tourner le dos au monde et de veiller sur ceux qu'elle aime. Il est difficile de décrire l'ambiance unique de ce jardin fleuri aux arbres séculaires et de cette grande terrasse ornée de vases Médicis qui surplombe un panorama dont la beauté ne cesse d'étonner Elisabetta. De son atelier sous les combles, dont elle a fait sa tour d'ivoire, elle contemple le Chianti et son Florence natal, lointain, et pense déjà aux créations qui s'échapperont bientôt de sous ses doigts avides de rêve.

LEFT: *Elisabetta Pandolfini at her work-table.*
FACING PAGE: *In the attic, Elisabetta has created a spacious, well-lit artist's studio.*

LINKS: *Elisabetta Pandolfini an ihrem Arbeitstisch.*
RECHTE SEITE: *Im Dachgeschoss der Villa hat sich Elisabetta ein geräumiges lichtdurch-flutetes »Künstlernest« geschaffen.*

A GAUCHE: *Elisabetta Pandolfini à sa table de travail.*
PAGE DE DROITE: *Sous les combles de la villa, Elisabetta s'est créé un nid d'artiste spacieux et inondé de lumière.*

RIGHT: *In the studio, a rough clay model for a sculpture awaits the skilled hands of Elisa-betta.*

RECHTS: *Im »studio-lo«, dem Atelier, wartet eine Rohskulptur aus Ton auf die geschickten Hände der Künstlerin.*

A DROITE: *Dans le « studiolo », une ébauche en terre glaise attend l'intervention de mains habiles.*

ABOVE: *In the dining room, Sunday lunch has come to an end and the guests have just risen from table.*

RIGHT: *Two terracotta totems by Elisabetta stand in the corner of the main drawing room.*

FACING PAGE: *Elisabetta is especially fond of yellow, which for her is synonymous with heat and sunshine. Yellow is the colour of the walls of her drawing room and the armchairs and soft, comfortable sofas in it.*

OBEN: *Im Esszimmer ist das Sonntagsessen beendet. Die Gäste haben gerade den Tisch verlassen.*

RECHTS: *Zwei von Elisabetta geschaffene Terrakotta-Totems recken sich in einer Ecke des großen Salons.*

RECHTE SEITE: *Elisabetta liebt die Farbe Gelb, die sie mit Sonne und Wärme verbindet. Ihre Lieblingsfarbe findet sich an den Wänden des Salons und in den Bezugsstoffen der behaglichen Couch und der Sessel.*

CI-DESSUS: *Dans la salle à manger, le déjeuner dominical vient de s'achever et les invités ont quitté la table.*

A DROITE: *Deux totems en terre cuite signés Pandolfini se dressent dans un coin du grand salon.*

PAGE DE DROITE: *Elisabetta adore le jaune, pour elle synonyme de soleil et de chaleur. Sa couleur favorite habille les murs du salon ainsi que les fauteuils et les canapés douillets et confortables.*

LEFT: *During the Thirties, Elisabetta's father Count Filippo (Pippo) Pandolfini installed the typically Art Deco bathrooms. His daughter has preserved them out of respect for him.*
FACING PAGE: *Souvenirs of a lifetime: on the mantelpiece, Elisabetta has assembled a sentimental still life.*

LINKS: *In den Drei-ßigerjahren ließ der Vater von Elisabetta, Graf Filippo Pandolfini – genannt »Pippo« – das Art-déco-Badezimmer installieren. Aus Respekt hat die Tochter nichts verändert.*
RECHTE SEITE: *Souvenirs, Souvenirs … Auf einem Kaminsims sammelt die Hausherrin Erinnerungsstücke.*

A GAUCHE: *Dans les années 1930, le père d'Elisabetta, le comte Filippo, dit « Pippo », Pandolfini, installa des salles de bains typiquement Art Déco. Par respect, sa fille n'y a pas touché.*
PAGE DE DROITE: *Souvenirs, souvenirs. Sur la tablette d'une cheminée, la maîtresse de maison a composé une nature morte sentimentale.*

PALAZZO BIZZAREI

Lucia e Giuliano Civitelli

Serre di Rapolano

The village of Serre di Rapolano, near Asciano in the Sienese Crete hills, is so named because for many years it formed a real barrier ("serra") against the invading Lombards. The proud castle of Serre di Rapolano and the stout buildings of its narrow streets still exude a relentless determination to oppose anything that might threaten the wellbeing and repose of those who live here. Lucia and Giuliano Civitelli bought the Palazzo Bizzarei in 1990. It is a narrow building dating from the Renaissance but with a mediaeval tower, and it stands in the shadow of the castle. The name is misleading, given that there is nothing at all odd about the Palazzo apart from the fact that it had been empty since the last war and that when the Civitellis took over they acquired not only the house but also all the furniture, curtains, crockery and linen that went with it. Other aspects which delighted them were the magnificent walled garden and a large number of period details – such as the great stone fireplace which dominates the kitchen, and the deep alcove in one of the bedrooms. Lucia Civitelli happily adopted the beautiful old curtains of embroidered linen and the white earthenware which she found in her new house. And since she adores simple, cool, sunny interiors, her Palazzo Bizzarei, so attractively transformed, now perhaps deserves the nickname of Palazzo Bianco or White Palace.

Giuliano and Lucia – who is pregnant with her first child – stand on the threshold of their walled garden.

Giuliano und Lucia, die ihr erstes Kind erwartet, am Eingang zum Garten.

Giuliano et Lucia, enceinte de son premier bébé, posent sur le seuil de leur jardin clos.

Das Dorf Serre di Rapolano, bei Asciano in den Hügeln der Crete bei Siena gelegen, verdankt seinen Namen der Tatsache, dass es lange Zeit tatsächlich eine Barriere – »serra« – gegen die Invasion der Langobarden darstellte. Das stolze Castello und die massiven Häuser in den engen Straßen zeugen noch heute von dem starken Verteidigungswillen der Bewohner. Lucia und Giuliano Civitelli erwarben 1990 den Palazzo Bizzarei, ein schmales Renaissance-Haus, das sich zu Füßen des Castello duckt. Trotz seines Namens weist das Gebäude mit dem mittelalterlichen Turm nichts »Bizarres« auf – sieht man davon ab, dass es seit dem Krieg leer gestanden hatte. So kamen die Civitellis auch in den Besitz der noch vorhandenen Einrichtung, der Vorhänge, des Geschirrs und der Wäsche. Besonderen Gefallen fanden sie an dem von einer Mauer umgebenen Garten ebenso wie an den originalen Architektur-Details, etwa dem Steinkamin in der Küche oder dem geräumigen Alkoven in einem der Schlafzimmer. Bei der Einrichtung des Hauses bediente sich Lucia der Fundstücke aus dem Haus, darunter wunderschön bestickte Leinenvorhänge und weißes Porzellan. Und da sie helle, klare Räume mag, könnte man Palazzo Bizzarei heute eigentlich umtaufen: in Palazzo Bianco.

One of the most charming corners of the house – a Romeo-and-Juliet balcony.

Eine der charmantesten Ecken des Hauses: ein Balkon à la Romeo und Julia.

Un des endroits les plus charmants de la maison: un balcon digne de Roméo et Juliette.

Le village de Serre di Rapolano, situé près d'Asciano dans la région des «crete senesi», doit son nom et sa réputation au fait qu'il a longtemps formé une vraie barrière – ou «serra» – contre l'invasion des Lombards. Le fier castello de Serre di Rapolano et les robustes bâtiments qui s'alignent le long des rues étroites, émanent encore cette détermination acharnée à combattre tout ce qui pourrait nuire au bien-être et au repos de ses habitants. Lucia et Giuliano Civitelli ont acheté le Palazzo Bizzarei – un étroit bâtiment datant de la Renaissance, agrémenté d'une tour médiévale et situé à l'ombre du château, en 1990. Contrairement à son nom, l'édifice n'avait de bizarre que le fait d'être abandonné depuis la dernière guerre. Les Civitelli, en devenant propriétaires, acquièrent aussi le mobilier, les rideaux, les faïences et le linge qui se trouvaient encore sur place. Ce qui les enchantait également, c'était la présence d'un exceptionnel jardin clos et le grand nombre de détails d'époque tels que la grande cheminée en pierre qui domine la cuisine et l'alcôve profonde dans une des chambres à coucher. Lucia, elle, n'hésita pas à intégrer les beaux rideaux de lin brodé et les faïences blanches trouvées dans sa nouvelle maison. Et comme elle adore les intérieurs simples, clairs et frais, son Palazzo Bizzarei, si joliment transformé, mérite plutôt le surnom de Palazzo Bianco.

The Palazzo Bizzarei seen from the tiny garden opposite.

Blick vom Gärtchen auf den gegenüberliegenden Palazzo Bizzarei.

Le Palazzo Bizzarei vu depuis le minuscule jardin d'en face.

LEFT: *a mouthwatering bowl of vine tomatoes and fresh garlic in the old marble sink.*
FACING PAGE: *In the kitchen, the accent is on rustic simplicity.*

LINKS: *Die Schale mit frischem Knoblauch und Strauchtomaten in dem alten Marmorspülbecken bieten einen appetitlichen Anblick.*
RECHTE SEITE: *Die alte Küche ist in schlichtem, rustikalem Stil gehalten.*

A GAUCHE: *Dans l'ancien évier en marbre, l'ail frais et les tomates en branches mettent l'eau à la bouche!*
PAGE DE DROITE: *L'ancienne cuisine respire la simplicité rustique.*

A LEFT: *The curtain, Thonet chair and wrought-iron washstand with its earthenware jug and basin were found in the house.*
FOLLOWING PAGES: *Art-Nouveau curtains provide a romantic touch in one of the bedrooms. The four-poster bed is of wrought iron, and the shape of the 1900 lampshade echoes the fresh-cut flowers in the vase.*

LINKS: *Der Vorhang, der Thonet-Stuhl und der schmiedeeiserne Waschstand mit Porzellangarnitur sind Fundstücke aus dem Haus.*
FOLGENDE DOPPELSEITE: *Jugendstil-Vorhänge geben dem Schlafzimmer ein romantisches Flair. Das Himmelbett ist schmiedeeisern, und*

der Lampenschirm von 1900 macht der hübschen Vase Konkurrenz.

A GAUCHE: *Le rideau, la chaise Thonet et le lave-mains en fer forgé équipé d'un broc et d'une cuvette en faïence, ont été trouvés dans la maison.*
DOUBLE PAGE SUIVANTE: *Rien de plus romantique pour une chambre à coucher que des rideaux Liberty. Le lit à baldaquin est en fer forgé et l'abat-jour de la lampe 1900 rivalise avec la fleur épanouie dans son vase.*

FACING PAGE: *The imitation marble in one of the bedrooms dates from the time of the original construction.*
RIGHT: *In one of the guest rooms, an Empire "bed with uprights" fills a deep alcove.*

LINKE SEITE: *Der »falsche Marmor« in einem der Schlafzimmer stammt aus der Entstehungszeit des Hauses.*

RECHTS: *Das Empire-Bett mit den hohen Pfosten hat seinen Platz in einem tiefen Alkoven in einem der Gästezimmer gefunden.*

PAGE DE GAUCHE: *Le faux marbre d'une des chambres date de l'époque de la construction.*
A DROITE: *Dans une chambre d'amis, un lit Empire à colonnes a trouvé sa place dans une alcôve profonde.*

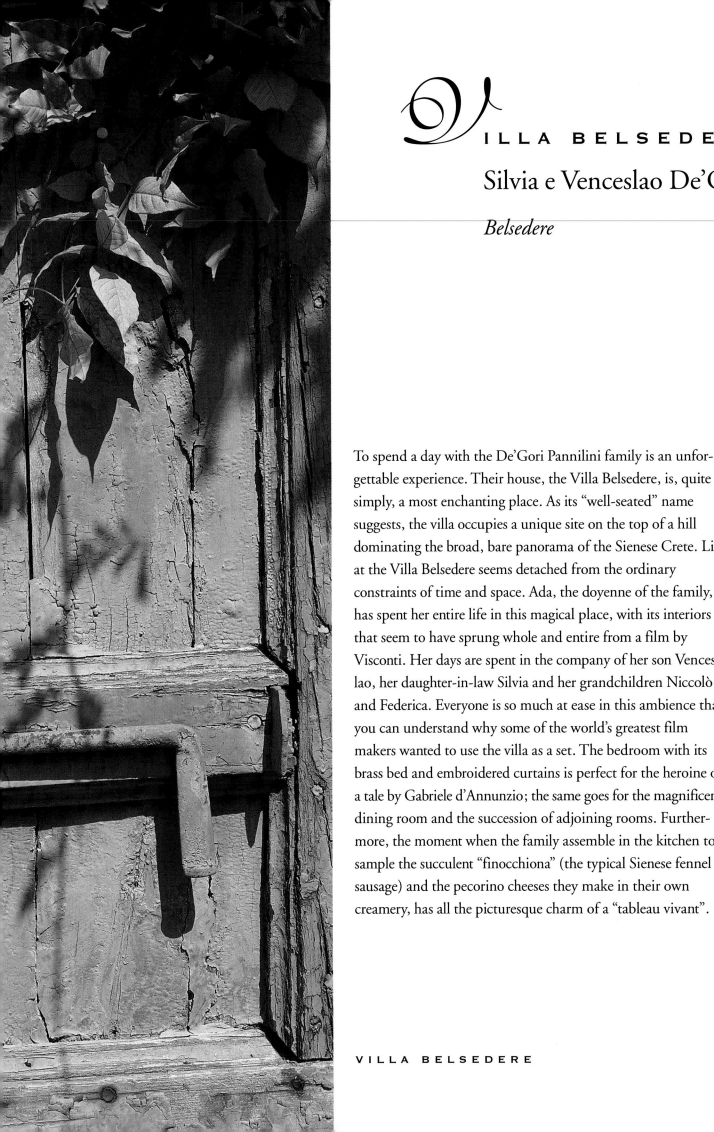

VILLA BELSEDERE

Silvia e Venceslao De'Gori Pannilini

Belsedere

To spend a day with the De'Gori Pannilini family is an unforgettable experience. Their house, the Villa Belsedere, is, quite simply, a most enchanting place. As its "well-seated" name suggests, the villa occupies a unique site on the top of a hill dominating the broad, bare panorama of the Sienese Crete. Life at the Villa Belsedere seems detached from the ordinary constraints of time and space. Ada, the doyenne of the family, has spent her entire life in this magical place, with its interiors that seem to have sprung whole and entire from a film by Visconti. Her days are spent in the company of her son Venceslao, her daughter-in-law Silvia and her grandchildren Niccolò and Federica. Everyone is so much at ease in this ambience that you can understand why some of the world's greatest film makers wanted to use the villa as a set. The bedroom with its brass bed and embroidered curtains is perfect for the heroine of a tale by Gabriele d'Annunzio; the same goes for the magnificent dining room and the succession of adjoining rooms. Furthermore, the moment when the family assemble in the kitchen to sample the succulent "finocchiona" (the typical Sienese fennel sausage) and the pecorino cheeses they make in their own creamery, has all the picturesque charm of a "tableau vivant".

In Tuscany, shutters with flaking paint are almost a badge of nobility!

Fensterläden mit abblätternder Farbe gelten in der Toskana als besonders edel!

En Toscane, avoir des volets à la peinture écaillée, c'est presque un titre de noblesse!

Ein Tag im Kreis der Familie De'Gori Pannilini ist ein unvergessliches Erlebnis, denn die Villa Belsedere besitzt einen ganz besonderen Charme. Wie ihr Name schon andeutet, liegt die Villa besonders schön auf einem Hügel und überragt die weite, karge Landschaft der senesischen Crete. Die Familie De'Gori Pannilini lebt hier friedlich und fernab von der betriebsamen Welt. Familienoberhaupt Ada hat ihr ganzes langes Leben an diesem magischen Ort verbracht. Sie verlebt ihre Tage mit Sohn Venceslao, Schwiegertochter Silvia und den Enkeln Niccolò und Frederica. Sie alle fühlen sich hier rundum wohl, und man kann gut verstehen, weshalb einige große Filmemacher die Villa und ihr nostalgisches Ambiente gerne als Filmkulisse genutzt hätten. Das Schlafzimmer, mit Kupferbett und bestickten Vorhängen, wäre die perfekte Umgebung für eine Heldin aus einem Roman von Gabriele D'Annunzio. Gleiches gilt für das geräumige Esszimmer und die Flucht der zahlreichen angrenzenden Salons. Sogar der Anblick, wenn sich die Familie in der Küche versammelt, um die köstliche »finocchiona«, eine mit Fenchel gewürzte Wurst, oder den selbst hergestellten Pecorino einzunehmen, lässt an eine poetische Filmszene denken.

Passer une journée au sein de la famille De'Gori Pannilini est une expérience inoubliable car leur décor quotidien, la villa Belsedere, possède un charme incomparable. Comme le suggère son nom, « la bien-assise » se dresse sur un site exceptionnel, et du haut de sa colline elle domine le vaste paysage dépouillé des « crete senesi », offrant à ses habitants le luxe d'une existence paisible que le temps ne semble pas concerner. Ada, la doyenne de la famille, a passé toute sa longue vie dans ce lieu magique; dans ces intérieurs qui semblent sortis tout droit d'un film de Visconti, elle partage ses jours avec son fils Venceslao, sa belle-fille Silvia et ses petits-enfants Niccolò et Frederica. Tous se sentent parfaitement à l'aise dans cette ambiance nostalgique et on comprend pourquoi les plus grands cinéastes du monde se battent pour tourner dans la villa. La chambre à coucher avec son lit en cuivre et ses rideaux brodés leur semble idéale pour héberger l'héroïne d'un roman de Gabriele D'Annunzio, et il en va de même pour la splendide salle à manger et les salons en enfilade. D'ailleurs, le moment où la famille se réunit dans la cuisine pour goûter à la succulente « finocchiona », le saucisson au fenouil typiquement siennois, et au pecorino qu'ils fabriquent dans leur propre ferme, possède tout le charme pittoresque d'un tableau vivant.

Everything has been jealously preserved in the old vaulted kitchen: the ovens, the rustic furniture, the copper utensils and even the patina on the walls.

In der Küche mit dem alten Gewölbe sind alle Gegenstände original: die Öfen, die soliden Möbel, die Kupfergerät- schaften und die schöne Patina an den Wänden!

Tout a été jalousement préservé dans l'ancienne cuisine voûtée: les fourneaux, le mobilier rustique, les ustensiles en cuivre et les murs joliment patinés!

PECORINO ALLA GRIGLIA

The De'Gori Pannilinis produce an excellent pecorino in their creamery, and nothing is easier to prepare – or more delicious – than "pecorino alla griglia":

Remove the rind of the pecorino with a sharp kitchen knife and cut into large slices about 1.5 centimetres thick. Allow one slice per person. Place the slices on a very hot grill, and toast till brown. Serve immediately, sprinkling with olive oil and pepper.

Die Familie De'Gori Pannilini stellen in ihrer »fattoria« einen exzellenten Pecorino her. Nichts ist leichter zuzubereiten – und schmeckt besser – als der »pecorino alla griglia«:

Entfernen Sie mit einem scharfen Messer die Rinde des Pecorino, und schneiden Sie den Käse in 1,5 Zentimeter dicke Scheiben. Rechnen Sie eine Scheibe pro Person. Die Scheiben werden auf den heißen Grill gelegt und so lange gegrillt, bis sich der Rost auf dem Käse abzeichnet. Mit etwas extranativem Olivenöl beträufeln, nach Belieben pfeffern und sofort servieren.

Les De'Gori Pannilini produisent un excellent pecorino, et rien de plus simple à préparer et de plus délicieux que le « pecorino alla griglia »:

Otez la croûte du pecorino avec un couteau à lame très fine et découpez-le en tranches d'un centimètre et demi d'épaisseur. Comptez une tranche par personne. Posez les tranches sur un gril très chaud, grillez jusqu'à ce que les marques du fer apparaissent sur le fromage. Servez immédiatement. Arrosez d'huile d'olive extra vierge et poivrez à volonté.

LEFT: *In this late 19th-century bedroom with its fine wrought-iron and brass bed, the atmosphere is vintage D'Annunzio.*

FOLLOWING PAGES: *Everything in the villa has echoes of the past. Even the electrical fittings date from an era when electricity itself was a novelty.*

LINKS: *Dieses Schlafzimmer mit dem schönen Bett vom Ende des 19. Jahrhunderts aus Schmiedeeisen und Messing wirkt so nostalgisch, als entstammte es einem Roman von D'Annunzio.*

FOLGENDE DOPPEL-SEITE: *Sogar die Elektroinstallation stammt aus der Zeit, als der Strom gerade seinen Einzug in die Wohnungen nahm.*

A GAUCHE: *Dans cette chambre à coucher fin de siècle, avec son beau lit en cuivre et fer forgé, règne une ambiance nostalgique à la D'Annunzio.*

DOUBLE PAGE SUIVANTE: *Même l'installation électrique date d'une époque où la fée Electricité venait de faire son entrée dans le monde.*

FACING PAGE: *The wallpaper in the antechamber dates from the 19th century, but the embroidery on the sofa is the work of Ada, the 88-year-old grandmother.*

RIGHT: *Family portraits surround a splendid Empire desk, an important piece by an unknown Tuscan cabinetmaker.*

LINKE SEITE: *Die Tapete im Vorzimmer stammt aus dem 19. Jahrhundert, aber die Stickerei auf der Couch ist das Werk von Ada, der 88-jährigen Großmutter.*

RECHTS: *Familienporträts umrahmen einen prächtigen Empire-Sekretär, ein Meisterwerk eines unbekannten toskanischen Kunsttischlers.*

PAGE DE GAUCHE: *Le papier peint de l'antichambre date du 19e siècle, mais la broderie sur le canapé est l'œuvre d'Ada, la grand-mère octogénaire.*

A DROITE: *Des portraits de famille entourent un splendide secrétaire Empire, œuvre majeure d'un ébéniste toscan inconnu.*

VILLA LE CARCERI

Val di Chiana

You spy it long before you reach it – a beautiful 16th-century villa with stout walls, square outlines, a small private chapel and a roof topped by a small edifice in which, they tell you, many gallons of sweet "vin santo" lie maturing. The villa's inhabitants, however, remain in the shade of the great cypress trees, or in the cool salons which protect them from prying eyes. For those privileged to enter, the house and its occupants have no secrets; the interior is warm and welcoming. The table in the dining room under its great billiard lamp is always loaded with good food and fine wines, and the kitchen is filled with the bright, cheerful voices of Ivana and Vera, the two maids. Le Carceri is filled to overflowing with family furniture and paintings. There is a bust inspired by Canova in an 18th-century corner niche, a steel Empire bed adorned with the gilded bronze head of an Egyptian and a kitchen in which the walls are hung with dozens of cake and jelly moulds made of copper. Is this the retreat of some grandee, or the lair of a wonderfully gifted decorator? We won't tell you – all we can say is that Le Carceri lives, breathes and sparkles despite its great age. And its most recent acquisition, a small drawing room adorned with a "trompe l'œil" vista painted by the distinguished painter Luchani is proof of it.

LEFT: *In one of the frescoes, a goldfinch is tempted by cherries.*
ABOVE: *Under the hand of the decorative artist, the walls of the small drawing room are steadily covered over with a "trompe l'œil".*

LINKS: *Ein gemalter Distelfink findet Gefallen an einigen Kirschen.*
OBEN: *Unter den begabten Händen des Kunstmalers sind an den Wänden im kleinen Salon erstaunliche »Trompe-l'œil«-Malereien entstanden.*

A GAUCHE: *Sur une des fresques, un chardonneret guette quelques cerises.*
CI-DESSUS: *Sous les doigts diligents du peintre-décorateur, les murs du petit salon se couvrent d'un trompe-l'œil étonnant.*

FOLLOWING PAGES: *The lovely facade is covered in a yellow-ochre wash. The road stretches away into the distance beneath the late afternoon sunshine.*

FOLGENDE DOPPELSEITE: *Einen schönen Anblick bieten das ockergelb gestrichene Haus und die Land-straße im weichen Licht der späten Nachmittags-sonne.*

DOUBLE PAGE SUIVANTE: *Quoi de plus beau qu'une façade couleur d'ocre et un chemin de campagne sous un doux soleil de fin d'après-midi?*

Schon von weitem erblickt man die zauberhafte quaderförmige Villa aus dem 16. Jahrhundert mit ihren dicken Mauern und der kleinen Kapelle. Unter der kleinen Maisonette-Haube auf dem Dach reift der milde »vin santo« heran. Die Bewohner halten sich lieber im Schatten der riesigen Zypressen im Garten oder in den kühlen Salons auf, wo sie vor neugierigen Blicken geschützt sind. Doch sie treten denjenigen, denen sie Einlass gewähren, offen und herzlich gegenüber. Warm und einladend wirken auch die Räume. Der Esstisch unter der eindrucksvollen Billardlampe ist stets reich mit auserlesenen Speisen und Weinen gedeckt, und aus der Küche dringen die fröhlichen Stimmen der Angestellten Ivana und Vera. Die Räume der Villa Le Carceri sind angefüllt mit Familienerbstücken und Gemälden. Da gibt es die von Canova inspirierte Marmorbüste, die auf einem Sockel aus dem 18. Jahrhundert thront, ein Empire-Bett aus Stahl, an dessen Kopfende ein vergoldeter ägyptischer Bronzekopf befestigt ist, und die Küche, deren Wände über und über mit kupfernen Kuchenformen bedeckt sind. Zeugt all das von einem adeligen Besitzer oder einem talentierten Innenarchitekten? Wir lüften das Geheimnis nicht. Die Villa Le Carceri lebt, atmet und sprüht vor Lebenslust – trotz ihres stattlichen Alters. Das beweist schon die jüngste Neuerung: ein kleiner Salon mit einer Gloriette, die von dem berühmten Luchani in »Trompe l'œil«-Manier mit einem Gartenlauben-motiv ausgemalt wurde.

On la voit déjà de loin, cette belle villa carrée du 16ᵉ siècle aux murs robustes, avec sa petite chapelle et son toit coiffé d'une maisonnette où mûrit le doux «vin santo», mais ses habitants préfèrent rester à l'ombre des cyprès et dans la fraîcheur des vastes salons qui les protègent des regards curieux. En revanche, pour ceux qui ont le privilège d'entrer ici, la maison et ses occupants n'ont pas de secret. Dans ces intérieurs, l'ambiance est toujours chaleureuse et accueillante, la table de la salle à manger surmontée d'une remarquable lampe de billard est toujours garnie de mets et de vins de qualité, et la cuisine résonne des voix gaies et claires des servantes Ivana et Vera. Qui dit Le Carceri évoque tout de suite l'image de tableaux et de meubles de famille, d'un buste en marbre inspiré par Canova placé sur une encoignure 18ᵉ, d'un lit Empire en acier orné d'une tête d'Egyptien en bronze doré et d'une cuisine aux murs recouverts d'une multitude de moules en cuivre. Repère d'un noble seigneur ou gîte d'un décorateur de talent? Nous ne dévoilerons pas son identité. Le Carceri vit, respire et pétille malgré son grand âge et la dernière acquisition, un petit salon orné d'une gloriette en trompe-l'œil peinte par le célèbre maestro Luchani, en est la preuve tangible.

LEFT: *Thanks to the virtuoso skills of the painter, the Tuscan landscape has entered the house.*

LINKS: *Ein virtuoser Maler hat die toska-nische Landschaft in das Haus geholt.*

A GAUCHE: *Grâce au talent du peintre, le paysage toscan est entré dans la maison.*

LINGUA AL DRAGONCELLO

Drop a calf's tongue into a saucepan of boiling salted water and cook for 45 minutes. Allow to cool, remove the skin from the tongue, season lightly with salt and pepper and replace in the boiling water to cook on a low flame for a further 1 1/2 hours. In the meantime, prepare a mixture of a handful of fresh, finely-chopped tarragon, two or three eggs whisked with a fork, half a cup of well-rinsed capers, a cup of stale bread soaked in the juice of half a lemon and a glass of red wine (don't let the bread mixture get too liquid), and four anchovy fillets crushed with a fork. Season this mixture with salt and pepper to taste and sprinkle freely with best-quality olive oil until the mixture takes on the consistency of a sauce. (Half a cup of oil should be sufficient.) Remove the tongue from the water, drain and carve into slices, cover the slices with the tarragon sauce and serve immediately.

Man legt eine Kalbszunge in kochendes Salzwasser und lässt sie 45 Minuten kochen. Die Kalbszunge abkühlen lassen, die Haut entfernen, leicht salzen und pfeffern und erneut ungefähr 1 1/2 Stunden ins kochende Wasser geben. Währenddessen mischen Sie einen Bund sehr fein gehackten frischen Estragon, zwei bis drei hart gekochte, gehackte Eier, eine halbe Tasse gut abgetropfte Kapern, eine Tasse altes Brot, das zuvor in dem Saft einer Zitrone und einem Glas Rotwein aufgeweicht wurde – achten Sie darauf, dass die Brotmasse nicht zu flüssig wird – und vier mit der Gabel zerdrückte Anchovisfilets. Die Mischung salzen, pfeffern und anschließend mit reichlich extra-nativem Olivenöl (eine halbe Tasse genügt) beträufeln, damit sie eine sämige Konsistenz erhält. Die Kalbszunge aus dem Topf nehmen, in dicke Scheiben schneiden, mit der Soße bedecken und sofort servieren.

Plongez une langue de veau dans une grande casserole d'eau bouillante salée et laissez-la cuire à feu moyen pendant trois quarts d'heure. Laissez tiédir, détachez la peau de la langue, salez et poivrez légèrement et replongez-la dans l'eau bouillante. Laissez cuire à feu très doux pendant une heure et demie environ. Pendant ce temps, mélangez une bonne poignée d'estragon frais finement haché, deux à trois œufs durs émiettés à l'aide d'une fourchette, une demi-tasse de câpres bien égouttés, une tasse de pain rassis trempé préalablement dans le jus d'un citron et un verre de vin rouge – veillez à ce que la préparation ne devienne pas trop liquide – et quatre filets d'anchois écrasés à la fourchette. Poivrez, salez et arrosez copieusement d'huile d'olive extra vierge jusqu'à ce que le mélange ait la consistance d'une sauce (une demi-tasse d'huile suffira). Otez la langue de la casserole, laissez égoutter, coupez-la en grosses tranches, nappez de sauce et servez immédiatement.

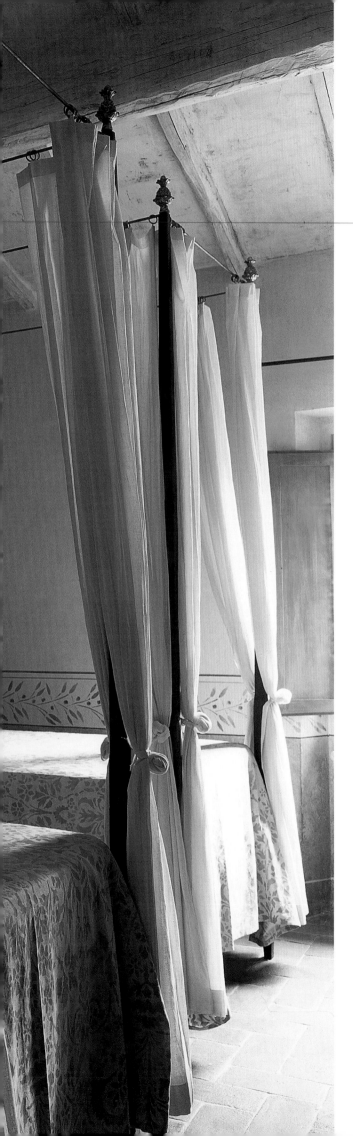

L'APPARITA

Cesare Rovatti

Val di Chiana

It takes time and effort to reach the second home of the Roman interior designer Cesare Rovatti south of Arezzo. The house is two hours by car from the capital, on top of a hill which is reflected on the clear surface of a lake. It is well worth the trouble. Originally L'Apparita was no more than a modest farmhouse, but with the advent of Rovatti and his taste for generous proportions it was quickly transformed into an imposing villa. From the outset, Rovatti's plan was to combine the ochre and burnt siena hues of Tuscany with the sober style of Scandinavia, and it is this which gives the place its originality and flair. Having openly set out to achieve a marriage between 18th-century Sweden and rural Tuscany, Rovatti was certainly daring in juxtaposing terracotta, tôle, wrought iron and earthenware pots with painted wooden chairs and a Gustavian chandelier. One must concede that the imitation marble, stencilled patterns, "trompe l'œil" panelling and hand-printed fabrics do add an unexpected note of lightness. Under the burning sun, against a background of murmuring fountains and surrounded by pine trees, cypresses and the stridulations of cicadas, all this makes for an atmosphere that is unusual, even fantastical. But after all, L'Apparita roughly translates as "she who looms up before your eyes".

In one of the bedrooms, the four-posters are lined up beneath a sloping ceiling.

In einem Schlafzimmer stehen Himmelbetten nebeneinander unter der Dachschräge.

Dans une des chambres à coucher, des lits à baldaquin s'alignent sous un toit en pente.

Der Innenarchitekt Cesare Rovatti fährt von Rom mehr als
zwei Stunden bis zu seinem Zweitwohnsitz südlich von Arezzo,
der Villa L'Apparita, die wunderschön über den stillen Wassern
eines Sees auf einem Hügel liegt. Ursprünglich war das Anwesen nur ein schlichtes kleines Landhaus, doch da Rovatti groß-
zügige Proportionen liebt, verwandelte er es schnell in eine ein-
drucksvolle Villa. Einerseits inspirierte ihn die sienarote und
ockerfarbene Palette der toskanischen Landschaft, doch gleichzeitig gibt es in den Räumen eine überraschende und originelle
nordische Note. Cesare Rovatti hat eine Vorliebe für rustikale
Möbel aus der Toskana, aber ebenso für Einrichtungsstücke aus
dem Schweden des 18. Jahrhunderts, und er hat keine Hem-
mungen, Terrakotta mit Blech oder Schmiedeeisen zu kombi-
nieren. Keramiktöpfe stehen hier neben bemalten Holzstühlen,
darüber hängt ein Kronleuchter im klassizistischen »Gustavian-Style«. Daneben finden sich falscher Marmor, Bordüren in
Schablonen-Technik, »Trompe-l'œil«-Vertäfelungen und hand-
bemalte Stoffe. In der brennenden Sonne, umgeben von Pinien
und Zypressen, haftet der ganzen Szenerie etwas Unwirkliches
an, besonders wenn im Hintergrund leicht die Brunnen
murmeln und in der Ferne die Grillen zirpen.

Il faut du temps et des efforts pour atteindre la seconde rési-
dence du décorateur romain Cesare Rovatti au sud d'Arezzo,
mais la récompense se trouve au bout de deux heures de voiture
de la capitale, au sommet d'une colline qui se mire dans les eaux
limpides d'un lac. Au début, L'Apparita n'était qu'un modeste
cabanon, mais grâce au talent de Rovatti et son goût pour les
proportions généreuses, elle se transforma en peu de temps en
une villa imposante, inspirée à l'évidence des ocres et des terres
de Sienne de la Toscane, ce qui ne l'empêche pas de flirter avec
la sobriété nordique qui lui confère une ambiance surprenante
et originale. Rovatti avoue qu'il a cherché à marier le 18ᵉ sué-
dois et la Toscane rurale. Il faut reconnaître qu'il n'a pas eu
froid aux yeux en combinant la terre cuite, la tôle, le fer forgé et
les pots en faïence avec des sièges en bois peint et un lustre
gustavien, et que les faux marbres, les décorations au pochoir,
les lambris en trompe-l'œil et les tissus décorés à la main apportent une note de légèreté inattendue. Sous le soleil brûlant, au
milieu des pins et des cyprès, avec en bruit de fond le murmure
des fontaines et le chant des cigales, cela tient à l'insolite et au
fantastique. Mais rien de surprenant à cela: après tout, L'Apparita signifie « celle qui est apparue devant vos yeux ».

LEFT: *Rovatti took care of every last detail – even the imitation marble and the ironwork are his own creations.*

LINKS: *Rovatti kümmerte sich auch um die kleinsten Details. Sogar der falsche Marmor und die Kunstschmiedearbeiten sind seine Entwürfe.*

A GAUCHE: *Rovatti s'est occupé de tout, et même les faux marbres et la ferronnerie portent sa signature.*

RIGHT: *Sunbeams linger on the stone steps leading to the first floor.*
FACING PAGE: *The loggia is ideal for alfresco lunches and dinners.*

RECHTS: *Die Sonne verweilt auf den Steinstufen, die in die erste Etage führen.*
RECHTE SEITE: *Die Loggia ist ein malerischer Ort für eine Mahlzeit »al fresco«.*

A DROITE: *Le soleil s'attarde sur les marches en pierre qui mènent au premier étage.*
PAGE DE DROITE: *La loggia est l'endroit idéal pour les repas al fresco.*

FACING PAGE: *In the salon, Rovatti used a sophisticated camaïeu palette. The beams are decorated with stencilled patterns, the panels and cupboards are painted in "trompe l'œil", and the pair of 18th-century marquise armchairs add a further note of elegance.*

ABOVE: *The designer has hung an 18th-century metal lantern above the table, which was made in Tuscany during the same period.*

LINKE SEITE: *Den Salon hat Rovatti raffiniert Ton in Ton gehalten. Die Deckenbalken sind in Schablonen-Technik bemalt, die Vertäfelungen und die Schränke sind »Trompe-l'œil«-Malereien, und die »Marquises«-Sessel aus dem 18. Jahrhundert geben dem Ganzen eine elegante Note.*

OBEN: *Über einem toskanischen Tisch aus dem 18. Jahrhundert hat der Innenarchitekt eine Metalllampe aus der gleichen Epoche angebracht.*

PAGE DE GAUCHE: *Dans le salon, Rovatti a eu recours à des camaïeux raffinés. Les poutres sont décorées au pochoir, les lambris et les armoiries sont peints en trompe-l'œil et la paire de marquises 18ᵉ apporte une note d'élégance.*

CI-DESSUS: *Au-dessus d'une table toscane 18ᵉ, le décorateur a accroché une lanterne en tôle de la même époque.*

LEFT: *The dining room is both countrified and sophisticated. The 18th-century chandelier is Gustavian.*
FACING PAGE: *The colours in the hall – ochre and grey – extend to the 18th-century chair and the stencil-decorated walls.*

LINKS: *Das Esszimmer ist gleichzeitig elegant und rustikal eingerichtet. Der Kronleuchter im »Gustavian-Style« stammt aus dem 18. Jahrhundert.*
RECHTE SEITE: *Die Farbgebung im Eingangsbereich – Ockergelb und Dunkelgrau – setzt sich in dem Stuhl aus dem 18. Jahrhundert und den Wandverzierungen fort.*

A GAUCHE: *La salle à manger est à la fois rustique et sophistiquée. Le chandelier 18ᵉ est gustavien.*
PAGE DE DROITE: *Les couleurs de l'entrée – ocre et gris – se retrouvent dans le siège 18ᵉ et les murs décorés au pochoir.*

RIGHT: *A "cotto" floor, a rustic table and chairs and a yellow cupboard with olive-green borders are the principal features of this welcoming kitchen.*

RECHTS: *In der einladenden Küche setzen ein Boden aus Terrakottafliesen, ein massiver Tisch und rustikale Stühle Akzente. Die gelbe Anrichte ist olivgrün abgesetzt.*

A DROITE: *Un sol en «cotto», une table et des chaises campagnardes et une armoire à rangements jaune avec des rechampis vert olive sont les éléments principaux de cette cuisine accueillante.*

LEFT: *The architecture of the bathroom has all the hallmarks of Rovatti – as do the tub, the old-fashioned fittings and the bull's-eye window above the door.*

LINKS: *Auch das Badezimmer trägt die Handschrift von Cesare Rovatti, der den Raum mit einer Badewanne und einem alten Waschbecken ausstattete. Über der Tür ließ er ein Ochsenauge anbringen.*

A GAUCHE: *La salle de bains porte la griffe du décorateur, en témoignent la baignoire et la robinetterie à l'ancienne, et l'œil-de-bœuf au-dessus de la porte.*

FACING PAGE: *In Cesare's bedroom, the vaulted ceiling is decorated with "trompe l'œil" panelling. The Piedmontese wardrobe is 18th-century, but the bed with its uprights is Cesare Rovatti's personal creation.*

RIGHT: *In this bedroom the walls and the counterpane are covered with a stencilled pattern inspired by the damask fabrics of Mariano Fortuny (1871–1949).*

LINKE SEITE: *Im Zimmer von Cesare schmückt eine » Trompe-l'œil«-Vertäfelung die gewölbte Decke. Der piemontesische Schrank stammt aus dem 18. Jahrhundert, doch das Bett mit den hohen Pfosten ist ein Entwurf des Hausherrn.*

RECHTS: *Die Gestaltung der Wände und der Tagesdecke in diesem Schlafzimmer ist einem Muster nachempfunden, das Mariano Fortuny (1871–1949) für Damaststoffe entwarf.*

PAGE DE GAUCHE: *Dans la chambre de Cesare, le plafond voûté est décoré d'un trompe-l'œil qui imite des lambris. L'armoire piémontaise est 18ᵉ mais le lit à colonnes est une création du maître de maison.*

A DROITE: *Dans cette chambre à coucher, les murs et le couvre-lit sont ornés d'un décor au pochoir inspiré des tissus damassés de Mariano Fortuny (1871–1949).*

EREMO SANTA MARIA MADDALENA

Marilena e Lorenzo Bonomo

Appennino umbro-toscano

Michelangelo is said to have come to Eremo Santa Maria Maddalena near Arezzo in 1556 to escape the wrath of the Pope, but the reason why Marilena and Lorenzo Bonomo live in this mediaeval hermitage on its steep hillside had nothing to do with the celebrated painter. The Bonomos are passionate lovers of contemporary art; in opening a gallery in Bari, Puglia, in 1971 they showed courage and foresight, given that the minimalist artists they revealed to the public in those early days had not yet achieved the international fame they presently enjoy. From the start Lorenzo, his wife Marilena and their daughters Alessandra, Gogo and Valentina were unstintingly generous and hospitable to their stable of unknown talents. Valentina – who is also an art promoter – remembers how the Eremo accommodated artists such as Sol LeWitt, Mel Bochner, Joel Fisher, Alighiero Boetti and Richard Tuttle under its roof. The artists have left traces of their passage in the form of graffiti, drawings, texts and mural paintings, so that today the hermitage has itself become a three-dimensional work of art. The furniture is largely of the minimalist type favoured by the Bonomos' protegés, though there are a number of austere pieces dating from the Middle Ages and the Renaissance which complement the modern art to perfection.

The façade of the former hermitage is distempered with a yellow-ochre wash made from natural pigments.

Die Fassade der ehemaligen Einsiedelei wurde mit ockergelber Farbe mit natürlichen Farbpigmenten gestrichen.

La façade de l'ancien ermitage a été badigeonnée avec un lavis ocre à base de pigments naturels.

The elevated site of the Eremo offers a breathtaking view of the landscape below.

Von Eremo hat man eine atemberaubende Aussicht auf die Landschaft ringsum.

L'emplacement de l'Eremo garantit une vue époustouflante sur le paysage environnant.

Angeblich hat Michelangelo 1556 vor dem Zorn des Papstes in der ehemaligen Einsiedelei bei Arezzo Schutz gesucht. Doch als sich Marilena und Lorenzo Bonomo entschlossen, das mittelalterliche Gebäude zu kaufen, das sich an einen steilen Hang schmiegt, hatte dies nichts mit dem Aufenthalt des berühmten Künstlers zu tun. Die Bonomos hegen eine Vorliebe für zeitgenössische Kunst, und sie bewiesen Weitblick und ungewöhnlichen Mut, als sie 1973 in Bari in Apulien eine Galerie eröffneten. Denn damals verfügten die Künstler der Minimal Art, die sie dem Publikum vorstellen, noch nicht über das heutige internationale Renommee. Großherzig und gastfreundlich boten Lorenzo, Marilena und ihre Töchter Alessandra, Gogo und Valentina in ihrem »Stall« unbekannten Talenten Unterkunft. Valentina, die übrigens ebenfalls Kunstberaterin ist, erinnert sich, dass unter anderem Sol LeWitt, Mel Bochner, Joel Fisher, Alighiero Boetti und Richard Tuttle in Eremo Santa Maria Maddalena wohnten. Die Künstler hinterließen Spuren in Form von Graffiti, Zeichnungen, Texten und Wandmalereien, sodass das entlegene Haus heute selbst zu einem dreidimensionalen Kunstwerk geworden ist. Für die Einrichtung ließen sich die Bonomos vom Minimalismus ihrer Schützlinge inspirieren. In Kombination mit einigen nüchternstrengen Möbeln aus dem Mittelalter und der Renaissance entstand ein Rahmen, in dem die Kunstwerke voll zur Geltung kommen.

On rapporte que Michel-Ange se cacha ici en 1556 pour échapper à la fureur du pape, mais la raison pour laquelle Marilena et Lorenzo Bonomo achetèrent cet ermitage médiéval aux alentours d'Arezzo, collé au flanc d'une colline en pente raide, n'a rien à voir avec le séjour supposé du célèbre génie. Les Bonomo éprouvent une véritable passion pour l'art contemporain et en ouvrant une galerie à Bari dans les Pouilles en 1971, ils ont fait preuve d'une perspicacité et d'un courage hors du commun, car les artistes minimalistes qu'ils présentèrent alors au public n'avaient pas encore la renommée internationale qu'on leur connaît aujourd'hui. Lorenzo, Marilena et leurs filles Alessandra, Gogo et Valentina offrirent l'hospitalité à leur « écurie » de talents inconnus. D'ailleurs Valentina – elle a, elle aussi, embrassé la carrière de promoteur d'art – se souvient que l'Eremo a logé, entre autres, Sol LeWitt, Mel Bochner, Joel Fisher, Alighiero Boetti et Richard Tuttle. Les artistes ont laissé ici des traces de leur passage sous forme de graffiti, de dessins, de textes et de peintures murales. Grâce à celles-ci, l'ermitage est devenu une œuvre d'art en trois dimensions. Côté mobilier, les Bonomo ont choisi la voie du minimalisme dictée par leur protégés, et des meubles sobres et sévères datant du Moyen Age et de la Renaissance accentuent on ne saurait mieux l'importance des œuvres d'art.

The former mediaeval cloister, which backs on to a wooded hillside, is surrounded by a beautiful formal garden.

Der mittelalterliche Kreuzgang schmiegt sich an einen bewaldeten Hügel.

L'ancien cloître médiéval, adossé au flanc d'une colline boisée, est entouré d'un très beau jardin formel.

LEFT: *In the kitchen, with its sturdy rustic chairs and table, the works of art on the mantelpiece carry the signatures of Alighiero Boetti, Joel Fisher and Sol LeWitt. The red cat on the right was painted by Eva LeWitt, Sol's daughter, as a child.*

FACING PAGE: *A stencilled mural by Boetti in the front hall forms a striking contrast with the Victorian armchair and the rustic furniture.*

LINKS: *Die Kunstwerke auf dem Kaminsims in der ländlichen Küche stammen von Alighiero Boetti, Joel Fisher und Sol LeWitt. Die rote Katze rechts ist eine Kinderzeichnung von LeWitts Tochter Eva.*

RECHTE SEITE: *Die Schablonenzeichnung von Boetti an der Wand im Eingangsflur bildet einen überraschenden Kontrast zu dem viktorianischen Sessel und den rustikalen Möbeln.*

A GAUCHE: *Dans la cuisine équipée de solides meubles campagnards, les œuvres d'art sur la tablette de la cheminée sont signées Alighiero Boetti, Joel Fisher et Sol LeWitt. Le chat rouge, à droite, est une œuvre de jeunesse d'Eva, la fille de Sol LeWitt.*

PAGE DE DROITE: *Dans l'entrée, une peinture murale de Boetti, exécutée au pochoir, contraste vivement avec le fauteuil victorien et les meubles rustiques qui l'entourent.*

LEFT: *In 1971, Sol LeWitt decorated the wall on one of the landings with a pencil wall-drawing of a network of "Circles from the Center".*
FACING PAGE: *A Romanesque font is now used as a wash-basin.*

LINKS: *Sol LeWitt zeichnete 1971 sein Werk »Circles from the Center« auf die Wand eines Treppenabsatzes.*
RECHTE SEITE: *Das Weihwasserbecken dient heute als Waschbecken.*

A GAUCHE: *En 1971, Sol LeWitt décora le mur du fond d'un des paliers en dessinant son œuvre «Circles from the Center».*
PAGE DE DROITE: *Le bénitier d'époque romane sert aujourd'hui de lave-mains.*

RIGHT: *The very sparsely furnished dining room inspired Mel Bochner to embellish the walls with the minimalist mural "Theory of Vision". The rustic furniture dates from the Renaissance.*

RECHTS: *Die Kargheit des Esszimmers inspirierte Mel Bochner zu der minimalistischen Wandmalerei »Theory of Vision«. Die rustikalen Möbel stammen aus der Renaissance.*

A DROITE: *L'aspect dépouillé de la salle à manger a incité Mel Bochner à décorer les parois de la peinture minimaliste «Theory of Vision». Le mobilier rustique date de la Renaissance.*

LEFT: *Painted cherubs stand guard over the sleeping inhabitants of this spartan bedroom. The rocaille looking glass dates from the 18th century.*
FACING PAGE: *The bathroom is built into a hollow of the rock against which the Eremo Santa Maria Maddalena is built.*

LINKS: *In diesem schlichten Schlafzimmer wachen auf Leinwand gemalte Engel über den Schlaf der Bewohner. Der Rocaillenspiegel stammt aus dem 18. Jahrhundert.*
RECHTE SEITE: *Das Badezimmer wurde in die Felswand gehauen, an die sich Eremo Santa Maria Maddalena stützt.*

A GAUCHE: *Dans cette sobre chambre à coucher, des angelots peints sur tôle veillent sur le sommeil des habitants. Le miroir rocaille est du 18e.*
PAGE DE DROITE: *La salle de bains est nichée dans la roche qui sert d'appui à l'Eremo Santa Maria Maddalena.*

IL ROMITO

Elisabetta e Claudio Naldini

Siena

There are times when Il Romito, the early 19th-century hermitage which stands in the Taya Grisaldi family's park at Il Serraglio, looks positively spectral in the morning mist. But as soon as the sun comes out, the old house shakes off all trace of ghostliness and becomes what it always was: a pretty, triple-arched, stone-built pavilion. Il Romito has acquired a new lease of life thanks to the magic wand of Elisabetta and Claudio Naldini, who out of respect for the maxim on the white marble pediment above the front door – "pulsate et aperietur vobis" (knock and it shall be opened unto you) – have flung wide the gates of their hermitage to their family and numerous friends. Although they only use the place as a summer retreat, the Naldinis have furnished it to withstand all seasons and weathers. The simple furniture, the bouquets of wildflowers gathered behind the house in the "bosco inglese" of cedars and sequoias – and the charming presence of an occasional devotional image – are all indicative of the Naldinis' approach to life. So is their table, which stands covered with a cloth of old cretonne and set for a delicious meal.

On a bedside table, someone has stuck an artificial rose behind the frame of a picture of the Sacred Heart of Christ.

Jemand hat eine künstliche Rose auf das Herz-Jesu-Bild auf dem Nachttisch gelegt.

Sur une table de chevet, quelqu'un a posé une rose artificielle sur le cadre d'une image pieuse représentant le Sacré-Cœur de Jésus.

Il Romito enveloped in
the mist of an autumn
afternoon.

Il Romito inmitten
von herbstlichen Nebel-
schwaden an einem
späten Nachmittag.

Il Romito … dans un
voile de brouillard dense
par une fin d'après-
midi d'automne.

An manchen Tagen hüllt sich Il Romito am Morgen in einen Schleier aus Nebelschwaden und wirkt dann wie eine Erscheinung aus einer anderen Welt. Doch sobald die Sonne den Dunst auflöst, verwandelt sich die ehemalige Einsiedelei bei Siena wieder zurück in einen hübschen Steinpavillon mit drei schmückenden Bögen. Das Gebäude, das aus der ersten Hälfte des 19. Jahrhunderts stammt, liegt einsam im Park des Anwesens Il Serraglio, das der Familie von Taya Grisaldi gehört. Heute hat Il Romito zu neuem Leben zurückgefunden, dank Elisabetta und Claudio Naldini, die sich dabei an die Maxime hielten, die auf einem weißen Marmorschild über dem Eingangsportal zu lesen ist – »pulsate et aperietur vobis«: Klopft und die Tür wird euch aufgetan. Elisabetta und Claudio halten die Türen weit offen für ihre Familie und ihre zahlreichen Freunde. Obwohl sie den Pavillon nur in den Sommermonaten bewohnen, haben sie ihn mit robusten Möbeln eingerichtet, die für alle Jahreszeiten tauglich sind. Hinter dem Gebäude befindet sich der Park »Bosco Inglese« mit gewaltigen Zedern und Mammutbäumen. Und im Haus sorgen ein Feldblumenstrauß, ein Heiligenbild und der reich gedeckte Tisch für ein nostalgisch-romantisches Ambiente.

Il y a des moments où Il Romito, enveloppé d'une chape de brouillard matinal, ressemble à une apparition fantomatique, mais dès que le soleil darde ses rayons, cet ancien ermitage construit durant la première moitié du 19e siècle dans le parc de «Il Serraglio» appartenant à la famille de Taya Grisaldi, secoue ses habits de spectre et redevient un joli pavillon en pierre orné de trois arches. Aujourd'hui, Il Romito est revenu à la vie grâce aux coups de baguette magique d'Elisabetta et Claudio Naldini. Ceux-ci, par respect pour la maxime qui orne le fronton en marbre blanc au-dessus de la porte d'entrée «pulsate et aperietur vobis» – frappez, et on vous ouvrira – ont ouvert tout grand les portes de leur ermitage aux membres de leur famille et à leurs nombreux amis. Bien que ce modeste pavillon ne leur serve que de maison de plaisance pendant les mois d'été, les Naldini l'ont meublé pour qu'il puisse faire face à toutes les saisons. Le mobilier robuste et simple, le bouquet champêtre cueilli derrière la maison – dans le Bosco Inglese où poussent des cèdres et même des séquoias – et la présence charmante d'une image pieuse ou d'une table nappée d'une vieille cretonne et chargée de plats succulents témoignent de leur penchant pour une ambiance teintée de bien-être, de nostalgie et de romantisme.

The rear of the house, with its disused chapel, overlooks the Bosco Inglese.

Hinter dem Haus befindet sich der »Bosco Inglese« mit einer »stillgelegten« Kapelle.

Donnant sur le Bosco Inglese, la partie arrière de la maison abrite une chapelle désaffectée.

PULSATE ET APERIETUR VOBIS

LEFT: *From this corner of the room, the gaze wanders out to the loggia. A hand brush and some copper vessels have been left on the chest of drawers, while the wall is hung with a collection of old kitchen utensils.*
FACING PAGE: *In the bedroom, breakfast is taken "tête-à-tête" on a folding bamboo table.*

LINKS: *Von dieser Zimmerecke geht der Blick nach draußen auf die Loggia. Auf der antiken Kommode liegt ein Handbesen neben Kupferkannen, und an der Wand hängt eine Sammlung alter Küchengeräte.*
RECHTE SEITE: *Im Schlafzimmer nimmt man das Frühstück »Tête à tête« an einem Klapptisch aus Bambus ein.*

A GAUCHE: *De ce coin de la pièce, le regard se pose sur la loggia à l'extérieur. Sur la commode ancienne, une balayette côtoie des vases de cuivre et une collection d'anciens ustensiles de cuisine est accrochée au mur.*
PAGE DE DROITE: *Dans la chambre à coucher, le petit déjeuner se déguste en tête à tête sur une table volante en bambou.*

$\mathcal{V}$ILLA VICO BELLO

Famiglia Anselmi Zondadari

Vico Bello

This house was built in the 16th century by the architect Baldassare Peruzzi for the very ancient family of Chigi-Zondadari. If you leave Siena and head northward in the direction of the residential suburb of Vico Bello, before long you will see in the distance the stark silhouette of the villa on the summit of a wooded hill. The surrounding area of Vico Bello is named after this villa with its dramatic terraced gardens; certainly Peruzzi, who endowed the house with a chapel, stables, an orangery and several pavilions, made the best of the view across the city to the Torre del Mangia and the Duomo. The arms of the Chigi family – six little mounds of stones with a star above – stand proudly above the terrace; there is a broad inner courtyard filled with boxed lemon and orange trees, and beyond these an architectural ensemble and a series of interiors that are uniformly elegant. Most enchanting of all is the collection of pastel-coloured frescoes and "trompe l'œils", representing sundry landscapes, diaphanous draperies, enigmatic sphinxes and indecipherable hieroglyphs. These serve as a backdrop to a wonderfully varied stock of furniture, lovingly assembled by generation after generation with an eye for beauty.

LEFT: *Goethe was right: it is good to be alive in "the land where lemons blossom".*
ABOVE: *Detail of a "mascherone" on one of the terracotta vases that adorn the terrace.*

LINKS: *Goethe hatte Recht: Im »Land, wo die Zitronen blühen«, lässt es sich gut leben!*
OBEN: *Detail eines »mascherone«, der einen der Terrakotta-Töpfe auf der Terrasse ziert.*

A GAUCHE: *Goethe avait raison: il fait bon vivre dans « le pays où fleurissent les citronniers » !*
CI-DESSUS: *détail d'un « mascherone » sur un des pots en terre cuite qui ornent la terrasse.*

Im 16. Jahrhundert wurde die Villa von dem bekannten Architekten Baldassare Peruzzi für die alte Adelsfamilie Chigi-Zondadari erbaut und mit einer Kapelle, Ställen, einer Orangerie und mehreren Pavillons ausgestattet. Wenn man von Siena aus nach Norden in Richtung des Dorfes Vico Bello fährt, entdeckt man schon von weitem am hügeligen, baumbewachsenen Horizont die strenge Silhouette der Villa, die der schönen Landschaft den Namen gab. Die Lage hoch oben auf einem Hügel und der in Terrassen angelegte Garten haben durchaus auch etwas Theatralisches. Von der Villa Vico Bello aus überblickt man Siena und hat eine fantastische Aussicht auf die Silhouetten der Torre del Mangia und des Duomo. Über der Terrasse ist das Wappen der Familie Chigi angebracht: sechs Hügel und ein Stern. Von dem großen Innenhof aus, in dem zahlreiche Töpfe mit Zitronen- und Orangenbäumen stehen, gelangt man in ein Ensemble elegant ausgestatteter Innenräume. Besonders bezaubernd wirken die Fresken und die pastellfarbenen »Trompe-l'œil«-Malereien. Sie bieten den passenden Rahmen für die äußerst unterschiedlichen Einrichtungsstücke, von Generationen von Bewohnern liebevoll und mit viel Sinn für Schönheit gesammelt.

Elle fut construite au 16ᵉ siècle par le célèbre architecte Baldassare Peruzzi pour la très ancienne et noble famille Chigi-Zondadari. En quittant Sienne vers le nord en direction du quartier résidentiel de Vico Bello, on aperçoit de loin, au sommet d'une colline boisée, la silhouette sévère de la villa qui prêta si gracieusement son nom aux alentours. La position de la Villa Vico Bello et de son jardin en terrasse mérite vraiment l'épithète de « théâtral », et Peruzzi, qui gratifia la demeure d'une chapelle, d'écuries, d'une orangerie et de plusieurs pavillons, était certainement conscient du fait que la vue sur la ville et sur les silhouettes de la Torre del Mangia et du Duomo, est l'un des atouts principaux de ce site exceptionnel. Les armes de la famille Chigi – six monticules en pierre surmontés d'une étoile – dominent la terrasse; de la vaste cour intérieure embellie par des rangées de citronniers et d'orangers en pots, on a accès à un ensemble architectural et à des intérieurs d'une très rare élégance. Ce qui enchante ici, ce sont les fresques et les trompe-l'œil couleur pastel, représentant des paysages, des drapés diaphanes, des sphinges énigmatiques et des hiéroglyphes indéchiffrables. Ils servent de décor à un mobilier hétéroclite, rassemblé avec amour par des générations successives d'occupants avides de beauté.

FACING PAGE: *In this room, the richly draped net curtain being lifted by sphinxes is a "trompe l'œil".*

ABOVE: *In this "salottino" the fine portrait of a woman above the fireplace is attributed to the celebrated English painter Sir Thomas Lawrence (1769–1830).*

RIGHT: *The pale colours of this small salon on the ground floor and the elegant white and gold furniture are reminiscent of Gustavian pastel tones.*

LINKE SEITE: *In einem der Salons sind die Wände mit einer » Trompe-l'œil«-Malerei aus großzügigen Drapierungen und Sphingen dekoriert.*

OBEN: *Das Frauenporträt über dem Kamin in diesem »Salottino« wird dem bekannten englischen Maler Sir Thomas Lawrence (1769–1830) zugeschrieben.*

RECHTS: *Die Pastelltöne im kleinen Salon im Erdgeschoss und die eleganten Möbel in Weiß und Gold erinnern an den »Gustavian-Style«.*

PAGE DE GAUCHE: *Ce voilage richement drapé que soulèvent des sphinges dans un des salons est un trompe-l'œil.*

CI-DESSUS: *Dans ce « salottino », le charmant portrait de femme au-dessus de la cheminée est attribué au célèbre peintre anglais Sir Thomas Lawrence (1769–1830).*

A DROITE: *Les pâles couleurs de ce petit salon du rez-de-chaussée et l'élégant mobilier blanc et or évoquent les tons pastel gustaviens.*

LEFT: *In one of the bedrooms a mahogany Empire bed is crowned by a canopy and surrounded by an extraordinary décor of hieroglyphs.*
FACING PAGE: *The shutters are closed and the room with the Egyptian frescoes lies in semi-darkness.*

LINKS: *Ein Baldachin krönt das prachtvolle Empire-Bett aus Mahagoni in einem der Schlafzimmer. An den Wänden ein ungewöhnlicher Hieroglyphendekor.*
RECHTE SEITE: *Die Fensterläden sind geschlossen, und das Zimmer mit den ägyptisierenden Fresken ruht im Dämmerlicht …*

A GAUCHE: *Dans une des chambres à coucher, le splendide lit Empire en acajou est couronné d'un baldaquin et entouré d'un étonnant décor d'hiéroglyphes.*
PAGE DE DROITE: *Les volets sont fermés et la chambre aux fresques à l'égyptienne somnole dans une lumière tamisée …*

PREVIOUS PAGES: *A magnificent "trompe l'œil" of landscapes, draperies, columns and antique vases covers the walls of the principal formal room.*
RIGHT: *One of the girls, Margarita, has just been married: her dress and veil have been left on the wrought-iron bed, in a room decorated with neo-classical frescoes.*

VORHERGEHENDE DOPPELSEITE: *Die Wände in diesem prunkvollen Salon ziert eine prächtige » Trompe-l'œil«-Malerei mit Landschaften, Drapierungen, Säulen und Vasen in antikisierendem Stil.*

RECHTS: *Eine der beiden Töchter, Margarita, hat gerade geheiratet, und ihr Brautkleid und der Schleier liegen noch auf dem schmiedeeisernen Bett in einem Schlafzimmer, das mit klassizistischen Fresken verziert ist.*

DOUBLE PAGE PRÉCÉDENTE: *Le grand salon d'apparat est décoré d'un splendide trompe-l'œil tout de paysages, de draperies, de colonnes et de vases « à l'antique ».*
A DROITE: *Une des filles, Margarita, vient de se marier et sa robe et son voile sont restés sur un lit en fer forgé dans une des chambres décorée de fresques néoclassiques.*

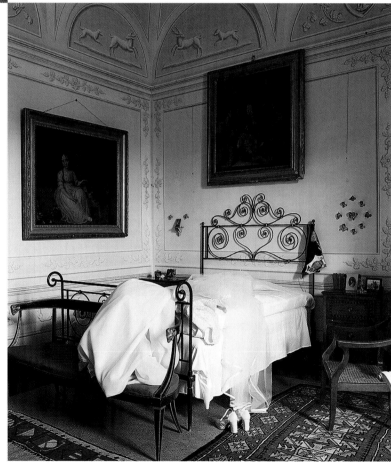

IL BELVEDERE

Laurie e Andrea Laschetti

Certano

Two years ago, Laurie and Andrea Laschetti and their daughter Flavia left Italy to go and live in Switzerland. But although they exchanged the green hills of Tuscany for the snowy mountain tops of the land of William Tell, they did not abandon their beautiful country home at Certano, near Siena. Il Belvedere, which they now use as a holiday retreat, has a stunning view across a valley filled with groves of olives, vineyards and sleepy farms. In the distance rise the towers of the celebrated Piazza del Campo, whose brightly-lit outlines stand out sharply at sunset against the night-blue horizon. Laurie is Irish and Andrea is from Rome; there is nothing pretentious about their house. What they wanted was a simple, uncluttered space, and in consequence Il Belvedere is furnished with rustic furniture and old-fashioned utensils of the kind used by the "contadini" (country people) who once lived in the house and worked the surrounding land. Here you will look in vain for any trace of sophistication. An ordinary white mosquito net covers the bed, which has an embroidered linen counterpane handed down in the family. The bedside bouquet consists of a few sage sprays arranged in an earthenware vase. And in the evening, the family gathers on the terrace to savour the delicacies concocted by "babbo" (Daddy), whose succulent "panzanella", bread salad, is the finest in the land.

LEFT: *the kitchen table, loaded with cheeses and a fine fresh bunch of basil.*
ABOVE: *Behind the house, the sun caresses the leaves of the vines.*

LINKS: *eine reichhaltige Käseplatte und frischer Basilikum auf dem Küchentisch.*
OBEN: *In den Weinbergen hinter dem Haus streicheln Sonnenstrahlen die Weinblätter.*

A GAUCHE: *Sur la table de la cuisine, un plateau de fromages et le basilic odorant mettent en appétit.*
CI-DESSUS: *Derrière la maison, le soleil caresse les feuilles des vignes.*

Vor etwa zwei Jahren verließen Laurie und Andrea Laschetti mit ihrer Tochter Flavia Italien und zogen in die Schweiz. Doch als sie die grünen Hügel der Toskana gegen die schneebedeckten Berggipfel im Land von Wilhelm Tell eintauschten, waren sie so klug, ihr schönes Landhaus in der Nähe von Siena zu behalten. Heute als Ferienhaus genutzt, bietet Il Belvedere einen atemberaubenden Blick über ein Tal mit Olivenhainen, Weinbergen und Bauernhöfen. In der Ferne sieht man sogar die Türme der berühmten Piazza del Campo von Siena. Laurie, eine Irin, und Andrea, der Römer, bevorzugen ein schlichtes Ambiente, und so gestalteten sie ihr Haus ohne jeden Prunk und Protz. Die Einrichtung mit den rustikalen Tischen und Stühlen sowie alten Küchengeräten lässt an die alten »contadini«, die Bauern, denken, die hier einst lebten. Über dem Bett hängt ein weißes Moskitonetz, darauf liegt bestickte Bettwäsche. Salbeizweige bilden ein hübsches Arrangement in einer Keramikvase, und das Sofa verbirgt sich unter einer gesteppten Baumwolldecke. Wenn die Familie den Tag gemeinsam auf der Terrasse ausklingen lässt, genießen alle die köstlichen kleinen Gerichte von »babbo« und lassen sich besonders die »panzanella«, toskanischen Brotsalat, schmecken!

Deux ans à peine que Laurie et Andrea Laschetti et leur fille Flavia ont quitté l'Italie pour aller vivre en Suisse. Mais s'ils ont échangé les collines vertes de la Toscane contre les cimes neigeuses du pays de Guillaume Tell, ils se sont bien gardé d'abandonner leur belle maison de campagne près de Sienne. Devenue désormais maison de vacances, Il Belvedere offre à ses hôtes une vue époustouflante sur un vallon parsemé d'oliviers, de vignobles et de fermes rustiques et sur les tours de la célèbre Piazza del Campo dont les silhouettes illuminées se détachent, le soir, sur l'horizon bleu nuit. La maison de Laurie l'Irlandaise et d'Andrea le Romain n'a rien de prétentieux, et comme ils la voulaient simple et dépouillée, ils l'ont garnie de meubles rustiques et d'ustensiles anciens liés étroitement à l'existence des anciens «contadini». Ici, on cherche en vain la sophistication: le lit est coiffé d'une simple moustiquaire blanche et habillé d'un linge de grand-mère brodé, le bouquet est fait de quelques branches de sauge arrangées dans un vase en faïence et le canapé est dissimulé sous une généreuse couverture en coton piqué. Le soir, la famille réunie sur la terrasse savoure les délicieux petits plats de «babbo» dont la succulente «panzanella» fait frémir les papilles!

In her modest kitchen, Laurie has prepared a light meal: tomatoes and cheese with a Montalcino wine. The olive branches in the earthenware jug form an unusual arrangement.

In ihrer einfachen Küche hat Laurie einen kalten Imbiss vorbereitet: Tomaten, Käse und Wein aus Montalcino. Das hübsche Bouquet im Keramikkrug besteht aus Olivenzweigen.

Dans sa cuisine modeste, Laurie a préparé un en-cas: tomates et fromages arrosés d'un Montalcino. Dans le broc en faïence, des branches d'olivier forment un bouquet surprenant.

LEFT: *There is nothing ostentatious in the decor of the living room. The whitewashed walls, woven baskets and opaline lamp are quite sufficient to create an atmosphere of comfort.*
BELOW: *Detail of a wrought-iron rail; the knocker on one of the doors.*

LINKS: *Einfach und schlicht: Weiß gekälkte Wände, geflochtene Körbe und eine Milchglaslampe schaffen eine behagliche Atmosphäre.*
UNTEN: *Detail eines schmiedeeisernen Treppengeländers; ein Türklopfer.*

A GAUCHE: *Rien d'ostentatoire dans la décoration du séjour. Les murs blanchis à la chaux, les paniers d'osier et la lampe en opaline suffisent à créer une ambiance douillette.*
CI-DESSUS: *détail d'une rampe en fer forgé; le heurtoir d'une porte.*

FACING PAGE: *In the bedroom a solid country bed with a mosquito net takes up nearly the whole room. The 18th-century chair was brought from Ireland.*

LINKE SEITE: *Das Bauernbett mit Moskitonetz nimmt fast das ganze Schlafzimmer ein. Der Stuhl aus dem 18. Jahrhundert ist ein Mitbringsel aus Irland.*

PAGE DE GAUCHE: *Dans la chambre à coucher, un solide lit campagnard couronné d'une moustiquaire prend toute la place. La chaise 18ᵉ vient d'Irlande.*

VILLA DI GEGGIANO

Alessandra Bianchi Bandinelli
e Ruggiero Boscu

Geggiano

The Villa di Geggiano rises from its lush surrounding land-scape like a dignified old lady covered in jewels and swathed in a sumptuous feather boa. The avenue of cypresses, elegant facade, "teatrino all'aperto" (open-air theatre), porticoes festooned with cherubs and "singeries" and the chapel imme-diately show that this is no ordinary place. The Bianchi Ban-dinellis, who built the house on much older foundations at the end of the 18th century, have a family tree that includes Pope Alexander III and a world-class archaeologist and art historian, Ranuccio Bianchi Bandinelli (1900–1975). The present owners of the Villa di Geggiano, Ruggiero Boscu and his wife Alessan-dra Bianchi Bandinelli, are passionate about the property and its vineyards, and have passed on their enthusiasm to their sons Andrea and Alessandro. Today the two brothers and their families have turned their backs on the stresses of life in the capital and settled at Geggiano among the frescoes by Ignazio Moder and furniture by Agostino Fantastici to look after their vines and preserve their incomparable inheritance.

Detail of the fresco in the entrance corridor.

Detail des Freskos im Eingangsflur.

Détail de la fresque qui orne le couloir de l'entrée.

Wie sich die luxuriöse Villa di Geggiano in der Landschaft erhebt, gleicht sie einer würdevollen alten Dame mit Juwelen und Federboa. Die zypressengesäumte Allee, die elegante Fassade, das kleine Freilichttheater »teatrino all'aperto«, die Kapelle, die Engel und die affenartigen Figuren am Eingangsportal – all dies lässt auf einen außergewöhnlichen Ort schließen. Die Familie Bianchi Bandinelli, zu deren Stammbaum auch Papst Alexander III. und der weltberühmte Archäologe und Kunsthistoriker Ranuccio Bianchi Bandinelli (1900–1975) gehören, ließ die Villa Ende des 18. Jahrhunderts auf den Grundmauern eines früheren Gebäudes errichten und hat sie seitdem hingebungsvoll instand gehalten. Die Liebe zu ihrer Villa und den Weinbergen hat sich von den heutigen Besitzern Ruggiero Boscu und seiner Frau Alessandra Bianchi Bandinelli längst auf ihre Söhne Andrea und Alessandro übertragen. Heute haben die beiden Brüder und ihre Familien dem stressigen Leben in Rom den Rücken gekehrt, um in Geggiano zu leben, umgeben von den Fresken von Ignazio Moder und den Möbeln von Agostino Fantastici. Sie verwalten ihr Weingut und die Ländereien und kümmern sich um ihr unvergleichliches Anwesen.

The classical beauty of the Villa di Geggiano has been preserved by the family like a precious gem.

Die klassische Schönheit der Villa di Geggiano wurde von der Familie wie ein kostbares Juwel gehütet.

La beauté classique de la Villa di Geggiano a été préservée comme s'il s'agissait d'un bijou précieux.

Telle une vieille dame très digne parée de ses bijoux et portant un somptueux boa de plumes, la villa di Geggiano émerge du paysage luxuriant qui l'entoure. Son allée bordée de cyprès, sa façade élégante, son « teatrino all'aperto », petit théâtre en plein air, ses portiques ornés de chérubins et de « singeries » et sa chapelle nous révèlent son caractère exceptionnel. La maison a été édifiée sur des vestiges plus anciens vers la fin du 18e siècle par la famille Bianchi Bandinelli dont l'arbre généalogique peut s'enorgueillir d'un pape, Alexandre III, et d'un archéologue et historien d'art, Ranuccio Bianchi Bandinelli (1900–1975), dont la réputation internationale n'est plus à faire. La famille s'occupe toujours avec le même dévouement de la demeure ancestrale, et les actuels propriétaires, Ruggiero Boscu et son épouse Alessandra Bianchi Bandinelli, éprouvent une telle passion pour la villa et ses vignobles qu'ils ont réussi à transmettre leur enthousiasme à leurs fils Andrea et Alessandro. Aujourd'hui, les deux frères et leurs familles ont tourné le dos à la vie stressante de la capitale et sont venus vivre à Geggiano entre les fresques d'Ignazio Moder et les meubles d'Agostino Fantastici, pour veiller sur les vignobles et, surtout, pour préserver un héritage incomparable.

The dogs also have villas, built to scale.

Die Hunde haben ihre eigenen Villen – in passender Größe!

Les chiens aussi ont une villa à leur taille!

PREVIOUS PAGES:
The visitor is greeted by the striking figures that inhabit the late 18th-century frescoes of Ignazio Moder.
FACING PAGE:
Towards the end of the 18th century, the Duke of Lorraine presented the Bianchi Bandinelli children with this superb wooden horse.
ABOVE: *The tapestry rooms contain magnificent painted furniture made in about 1790, though the "tapestries" in question are no more than large canvases.*

VORHERGEHENDE DOPPELSEITE: *Schon am Eingang erwarten den Besucher die Fresken von Ignazio Moder vom Ende des 18. Jahrhunderts.*
LINKE SEITE: *Gegen Ende des 18. Jahrhunderts schenkte der Herzog von Lothringen den Kindern der Familie Bianchi Bandinelli dieses wunderbare Holzpferd.*
OBEN: *Im »Gobelin-Salon« stehen herrlich bemalte Möbel von 1790. Die »Gobelins« entpuppen sich allerdings bei näherem Hinsehen als gemalt.*

DOUBLE PAGE PRÉ-CÉDENTE: *Le visiteur est accueilli dès l'entrée par les personnages qui peuplent les fresques peint vers la fin du 18ᵉ siècle par Ignazio Moder.*
PAGE DE GAUCHE: *Ce superbe cheval en bois sculpté polychrome a été offert par le duc de Lorraine aux enfants des Bianchi Bandinelli vers la fin du 18ᵉ siècle.*
CI-DESSUS: *Le salon des Gobelins abrite un magnifique mobilier peint exécuté vers 1790, mais les gobelins ne sont en réalité que de grandes toiles peintes.*

ABOVE: *the celebrated "ciarlatorio" decorated by the Sienese painter Agostino Fantastici (1782–1849). This room, which has the proportions of a corridor, was a place to gossip.*
RIGHT: *The entrance to the house, with its large fanlight.*

OBEN: *Das berühmte »ciarlatorio« malte der senesische Maler Agostino Fantastici (1782–1849) aus. Es besteht aus einem flurartigen Raum, in dem man sich früher der Konversation widmete.*

RECHTS: *die Eingangstür mit einem Oberlicht in Fächerform.*

CI-DESSUS: *Le célèbre «ciarlatorio» décoré par le peintre siennois Agostino Fantastici (1782–1849), une pièce en forme de couloir où l'on s'adonnait jadis à l'art du commérage.*
A DROITE: *la porte d'entrée avec son lanterneau en forme d'éventail.*

RIGHT: *In the Blue Salon the walls are covered with wallpaper from the famous Paris store "Au Grand Balcon".*
FOLLOWING PAGES: *Sienese cabinet makers of the late 18th century decorated these pieces of furniture like porcelain, in blue and white. The fan and the small electric lamp, which are delicately matched with the wallpaper, both date from the early 20th century.*

RECHTS: *Die Tapete im Blauen Salon stammt aus dem berühmten Pariser Geschäft »Au Grand Balcon«.*
FOLGENDE DOPPELSEITE: *Kunstschreiner aus Siena verzierten gegen Ende des 18. Jahrhunderts die Möbel mit blauweißem Dekor, der an Porzellan denken lässt. Der Fächer und die kleine Lampe sind farblich auf die Tapete abgestimmt. Sie stammen beide vom Anfang des 20. Jahrhunderts.*

A DROITE: *Dans le Salon bleu, le papier peint des murs provient du célèbre magasin parisien « Au Grand Balcon ».*
DOUBLE PAGE SUIVANTE: *Des ébénistes siennois de la fin du 18ᵉ siècle décorèrent le mobilier en imitant la porcelaine bleue et blanche. L'éventail et la petite lampe électrique délicatement assortie au papier peint datent du début du 20ᵉ siècle.*

LEFT: *From one of the windows on the first floor there is a fine view of the "teatro all'aperto".*
FACING PAGE: *In the private chapel, the decor shows the Bianchi Bandinelli's taste for luxury and elegance.*

LINKS: *Von einem der Fenster in der ersten Etage hat man einen guten Blick auf das »teatro all'aperto«.*
RECHTE SEITE: *In der Privatkapelle zeugt die prächtige Ausgestaltung vom erlesenen Geschmack der Familie Bianchi Bandinelli.*

A GAUCHE: *D'une des fenêtres du premier étage, on peut admirer le « teatro all'aperto ».*
PAGE DE DROITE: *Dans la chapelle privée, le décor témoigne du goût des Bianchi Bandinelli pour le faste élégant.*

RIGHT: *In this bedroom the playwright Vittorio Alfieri (1749–1803) – who was a frequent house guest – spent many nights in the superb silk-hung four-poster bed.*

RECHTS: *In diesem Zimmer schlief der Dramatiker Vittorio Alfieri (1749–1803), der häufig zu Gast war, unter einem seidenen Betthimmel.*

A DROITE: *L'auteur dramatique Vittorio Alfieri (1749–1803) passa souvent la nuit dans ce superbe lit à baldaquin drapé de soie.*

$\mathscr{P}$ODERE TAVOLETO

Buonconvento

They moved into the big farmhouse of Podere Tavoleto in the early Forties and they've stayed there ever since: nine members of the same family, all real "contadini". Il Podere dates from the end of the 19th century. It is a square brick construction boasting a fine three-arched loggia, with outbuildings, piggeries, stables and vineyards beyond. Observing this united, patiently hardworking family going about their daily existence amid these surroundings, it is hard to avoid the conclusion that time has come to a dead halt at Il Podere Tavoleto. In the kitchen, "la mamma" is peeling potatoes, while keeping a careful eye on the "passata di pomodoro", tomato sauce, simmering on the venerable wood-fired range. "La nonna" and her granddaughter are busy preparing a meal for Grandpa, who is in his nineties, while out on the porch the imperturbable aunt shells her way through a mountain of broad beans. The younger brother takes care of the pigs, the hens, the turkeys and the light-coloured cattle, which are the chief glory of this beautiful region. "Spaventa-passeri" – scarecrows – sway in the wind above the rows of vines, and soon it will be time for "la cena", when all the family will come together around the table to drink a glass or two of cool sparkling wine and dine on the delicious food prepared by the women from recipes passed down the generations.

The farmers hang their working clothes in the porch when they come in from the fields.

Nach der Feldarbeit hängen die Bauern ihre Arbeitskleidung am Eingang auf.

Au retour des champs, les fermiers accrochent leurs vêtements de travail sous le porche.

Anfang der Vierzigerjahre zog die Bauernfamilie auf das große Gut Podere Tavoleto. Als echte »contadini« sind die neun Familienmitglieder in ihrer Heimat tief verwurzelt. Das »podere«, das Landgut, stammt vom Ende des 19. Jahrhunderts und besteht aus einem quaderförmigen, aus Ziegelsteinen errichteten Haupthaus, das mit einer Loggia mit drei Bögen geschmückt ist, sowie den Nebengebäuden, den Ställen, dem »porcile«, dem Schweinstall, und natürlich den Weinbergen. Wenn man die ganze Familie Hand in Hand arbeiten sieht, hat man den Eindruck, die Zeit sei stehengeblieben. Die »mamma« schält in der Küche Kartoffeln, die »nonna« und ihre Enkelin kümmern sich um das Essen für den 90-jährigen »nonno«. Die unerschütterliche »zia«, die Tante, schnippelt draußen einen Berg Bohnen, während der jüngste Bruder über das Wohl der Schweine, Hühner, Puten und der weißen Kühe wacht. Die »spaventa-passeri«, die Vogelscheuchen, wiegen sich im Wind über den Weinstöcken, und bald naht die Stunde des Abendessens. Dann versammelt sich die ganze Familie um den Tisch, um sich den kühlen Weißwein und die köstlichen Gerichte schmecken zu lassen, die die Frauen nach den Rezepten ihrer Großmütter zubereitet haben.

The three classical arches of the porch are worthy of a palace.

Der Eingang des Podere Tavoleto ist wie bei einem Palazzo mit drei klassischen Bögen verziert.

Le porche comporte trois arches classiques à la façon des palazzi.

The herd of blond-coloured cattle, typical of this part of the world, waiting to be fed.

Die für diese Region typischen weißen Kühe warten auf die Fütterung!

Les vaches blondes, si typiques de cette région, attendent l'heure du repas!

Ils s'installèrent dans la grande ferme du Podere Tavoleto à l'aube des années 1940 et ils y sont restés: neuf membres de la même famille, des « contadini » authentiques, ancrés à leur terre natale, que passionne la lutte parfois inégale entre l'homme et la nature. Le « podere » date de la fin du 19e siècle. Autour d'une construction carrée en briques, ornée d'une loggia embellie par trois arches, on aperçoit les dépendances, la porcherie, les étables et les vignobles et, en regardant vivre cette famille unie et laborieuse, on a l'impression que le temps s'est arrêté. La « mamma » épluche les pommes de terre dans la cuisine, promenant un œil vigilant sur la « passata di pomodoro » qui mijote sur l'ancienne cuisinière à bois, la « nonna » et sa petite-fille s'occupent du repas du grand-père nonagénaire, la « zia », la tante imperturbable, trie une montagne de fèves sous le porche et le frère cadet veille au bien-être des cochons, des poules, des dindes et des vaches blondes qui font la fierté de cette belle région. Le vent berce les « spaventa-passeri » – des épouvantails – au-dessus des rangées de vignes. Bientôt ce sera l'heure de la «cena» et toute la famille se réunira autour de la table pour goûter au petit vin blanc pétillant et frais et aux plats savoureux que les femmes ont préparés d'après les recettes et les rites de leurs aïeules.

LEFT: *The elder sister sifts patiently through a pile of "cannellini" beans which will later be used for succulent "fagioli all'uccelletto".*
FACING PAGE: *La Mamma has decreed that today the family will dine on gnocchi.*

LINKS: *Die älteste Schwester putzt geduldig die Bohnen, aus denen die köstlichen »fagioli all'uccelletto« zubereitet werden.*
RECHTE SEITE: *Die »mamma« hat beschlossen, dass es heute »gnocchi« gibt.*

A GAUCHE: *La sœur aînée trie patiemment les « cannellini », des haricots, qui serviront à préparer les succulents « fagioli all'uccelletto ».*
PAGE DE DROITE: *La « mamma » a décidé que sa famille mangerait des « gnocchi » aujourd'hui.*

PREVIOUS PAGES: *The grape harvest will begin any day now, and at Il Podere Tavoleto preparations for the "festa dell'uva" are already well in hand. A rooster moulded out of cement stands in the centre of the farmyard.*
RIGHT: *A large pot filled with "pappa al pomodoro" simmers on the old wood stove, filling the kitchen with delicious smells.*

VORHERGEHENDE DOPPELSEITE: *Die Zeit der Weinernte naht und auf Podere Tavoleto freut man sich auf die »festa dell'uva« … Ein stolzer Hahn aus Zement bewacht den Hof.*
RECHTS: *Ein randvoll gefüllter Topf mit »pappa al pomodoro« köchelt auf dem alten Kohleherd und verströmt einen köstlichen Duft.*

DOUBLE PAGE PRÉCÉDENTE: *La saison des vendanges approche et avec elle la « festa dell'uva » … Un coq en ciment garde la basse-cour.*
A DROITE: *Une grande casserole remplie de purée de tomates cuit à petit feu, et son odeur met l'eau à la bouche.*

FAGIOLI ALL'UCCELLETTO

This is a typically Tuscan winter dish based on "cannellini" white beans:

Leave the dry beans to soak overnight in cold water. In the morning, drain the beans, place in a large casserole, pour in just enough cold water to cover, then add a tablespoon of olive oil and some fresh sage. Bring to the boil and simmer till the beans are soft and creamy. Drain the beans, discarding the sage, and allow to cool. Heat several tablespoons of the finest olive oil in a cast-iron stew-pan, then add one clove of garlic, a few sage leaves and one tomato, skinned and diced, per person. Simmer this mixture on a very low flame for half an hour, add the beans and simmer for a further twenty minutes. Serve piping hot, sprinkled with finely-chopped fresh sage leaves.

Note: If pre-cooked canned beans are used, simmer for five minutes only and add to the tomato mixture at the last minute.

Dies ist ein typisch toskanisches Wintergericht mit weißen Bohnen, die »cannellini« genannt werden:

Die getrockneten weißen Bohnen werden über Nacht in Wasser eingeweicht. Am nächsten Tag lässt man sie in einem großen Topf kochen, wobei sie gerade mit Wasser bedeckt sein sollen. Dabei fügt man einen Esslöffel extra-natives Olivenöl und einige Salbeiblätter hinzu. Danach die Salbeiblätter entfernen und die Bohnen abtropfen und abkühlen lassen. Einige Esslöffel Olivenöl in einem gusseisernen Schmortopf erhitzen, pro Person eine Knoblauchzehe, einige Salbeiblätter und eine gehäutete und gewürfelte Tomate hinzufügen. Bei sehr schwacher Hitze eine halbe Stunde schmoren, die Bohnen hinzufügen und bei geschlossenem Deckel ungefähr zwanzig Minuten weiter köcheln. Mit klein gehackten Salbeiblättern bestreuen und sehr heiß servieren. Guten Appetit!

Wenn Sie weiße Dosenbohnen verwenden, sollten Sie sie nicht länger als fünf Minuten kochen und erst in letzter Minute hinzufügen.

A la base de cette recette d'hiver typiquement toscane, il y a les haricots blancs, les « cannellini » :

En général les haricots séchés ont été mis à tremper la veille. Cuisez-les alors dans une grande casserole, à peine recouverts d'eau pour qu'ils absorbent tout juste le liquide nécessaire. Ajoutez une cuiller d'huile d'olive et quelques feuilles de sauge. Egouttez-les, enlevez la sauge et laissez tiédir. Chauffez quelques cuillerées d'huile d'olive extra vierge dans une cocotte en fonte, ajoutez une gousse d'ail, quelques feuilles de sauge et une tomate pelée, coupée en dés, par personne. Laissez mijoter à feu très doux pendant une demi-heure, ajoutez les haricots, couvrez et laissez mijoter encore une vingtaine de minutes. Servez très chaud et saupoudrez de sauge finement hachée. Bon appétit !

Si vous utilisez des haricots blancs en conserve, ajoutez-les au dernier moment et ne les laissez pas mijoter plus de cinq minutes.

VILLA MONTOSOLI

Maria Carla Carratelli e Giorgio Leonini

Montalcino

The Villa Montosoli is truly majestic, but since it is hidden behind a wall at the end of an avenue of laurels, few outsiders ever glimpse its facade or its tall glassed-in loggia. The villa stands on the site of a former "castello"; it was built for the Tuti family in 1535 by the celebrated architect Baldassare Peruzzi, and for the last thirty years it has been the home of the antiques dealer Giorgio Leonini and his wife Carla, a gifted restorer of old masters. Over the years it has witnessed the arrival of three Leonini daughters, Alice, Claudia and Giovanna, while slowly filling up with an impressive number of paintings, furniture, statues, objects and cats. What makes the Leoninis' interior so nice is their nonchalant habit of combining very valuable furniture and pictures with the ordinary flotsam of daily life. They don't stand on ceremony. In the "salotto", which is decorated with neo-classical frescoes, they, their cats and their friends keep company without a trace of formality, and when Carla and her daughters have set the table in the small, shady courtyard and Giorgio is ready to serve his celebrated "zuppa di pane", bread soup, the Villa Montosoli fills with a sense of gaiety that is palpably Renaissance.

Under the arches of the portico, a superb plaster Venus awaits admittance into the "piano nobile".

Unter dem Eingangsportal wartet eine exquisite Venus aus Gips darauf, ins »piano nobile« vorgelassen zu werden.

Sous les arches du porche, une superbe Vénus en plâtre attend d'être admise au « piano nobile ».

Behind the Villa Montosoli, the horse eats his daily bucket of feed.

Hinter der Villa Montosoli nimmt das Pferd seine Ration Hafer in Empfang.

Derrière la Villa Montosoli, le cheval vient de recevoir son picotin.

Majestätisch wirkt sie, die Villa Montosoli, aber da sie sich hinter einer Mauer am Ende einer lorbeergesäumten Allee verbirgt, bleibt die prächtige Fassade mit der verglasten hohen Loggia den Passanten verborgen. 1535 wurde die Villa von dem berühmten Architekten Baldassare Peruzzi für die Familie Tuti an der Stelle eines alten Castello errichtet. Der Antiquitätenhändler Giorgio Leonini und seine Frau Carla, eine sehr begabte Gemälderestauratorin, wohnen seit dreißig Jahren hier, und in dieser Zeit hat die Villa die Geburt von drei Töchtern miterlebt: Alice, Claudia und Giovanna. Und mit ihnen kamen nach und nach eine Vielzahl von Gemälden, Möbeln, Statuen, Objekten und … Katzen ins Haus. Besonders sympathisch wirkt das Ambiente durch die unbekümmert-nonchalante Mischung aus wertvollen Möbeln und Gemälden sowie der typisch-chaotischen Unordnung, die im Alltag entsteht. Bei den Leoninis geht es nicht förmlich zu. Im »salotto« mit den klassizistischen Fresken muss keine Etikette beachtet werden, denn die Bewohner, die Katzen und die Freunde legen darauf keinen Wert. Und trotzdem: Wenn Carla und ihre Töchter den Tisch in dem kleinen schattigen Innenhof decken und Giorgio sich anschickt, seine berühmte Brotsuppe, »zuppa di pane«, zu servieren, verbreitet sich in der Villa Montosoli, wie zur Zeit der Renaissance, eine festliche Stimmung.

La Villa Montosoli est vraiment majestueuse, mais comme elle est cachée derrière un mur au bout d'une allée bordée de lauriers, elle ne révèle pas le spectacle de sa façade, ornée d'une haute loggia vitrée, aux passants en quête de beauté. L'antiquaire Giorgio Leonini et sa femme Carla, qui restaure avec talent les tableaux anciens, habitent depuis trente ans cette maison construite en 1535 sur l'emplacement d'un ancien castello par le célèbre architecte Baldassare Peruzzi pour la famille Tuti. Pendant ces trois décennies, trois filles, Alice, Claudia, et Giovanna ont vu le jour, et la demeure s'est remplie petit à petit d'un nombre impressionnant de tableaux, de meubles, de statues, d'objets et … de chats ! Ce qui rend l'intérieur des Leonini si sympathique, c'est la manière quasi nonchalante dont les meubles et les tableaux de grande valeur cohabitent avec le désordre chaotique lié à la vie de tous les jours. Chez les Leonini, on se rie des formalités. Dans le «salotto» décoré de fresques néoclassiques, les habitants, les chats et les amis tirent la langue à l'étiquette, et lorsque Carla et ses filles ont dressé la table dans la petite cour ombragée et que Giorgio s'apprête à servir sa célèbre « zuppa di pane », la Villa Montosoli, comme au temps de la Renaissance, prend un air de fête.

The avenue leading up to the villa is shaded by laurels.

Die lorbeergesäumte Allee führt zur Villa.

L'allée qui mène à la villa est bordée de lauriers.

FACING PAGE: *The walls of the drawing room are covered in neoclassical frescoes dating from the late 18th century.*

ABOVE AND RIGHT: *According to Giorgio Leonini, under these 18th-century frescoes lurk original paintings by Il Sodoma (1477–1549), a contemporary of Raphael.*

FOLLOWING PAGES: *In these rooms with their peeling walls, the Leoninis live their everyday lives surrounded by superb collections of objects.*

LINKE SEITE: *Die Wände des Salons schmücken klassizistische Fresken des späten 18. Jahrhunderts.*

OBEN UND RECHTS: *Unter den Fresken des 18. Jahrhunderts verbergen sich laut Giorgio Originalfresken des Malers Il Sodoma (1477–1549), einem Zeitgenossen von Raffael.*

FOLGENDE DOPPELSEITE: *Die abblätternde Farbe verleiht den Räumen Patina. Hier verbringen die Leoninis ihre Tage, umgeben von erlesenen Möbeln und Gemälden.*

PAGE DE GAUCHE: *Les fresques néoclassiques du salon datent de la fin du 18e siècle.*

CI-DESSUS ET À DROITE: *Selon Giorgio, les fresques 18e recouvrent les fresques originales peintes par Il Sodoma (1477–1549), un contemporain de Raphaël.*

DOUBLE PAGE SUIVANTE: *Dans ces pièces aux murs craquelés, les Leonini vivent parmi des objets de collection superbes et un amoncellement de meubles et de tableaux de grande qualité.*

LEFT: *In Carla's bedroom, an elaborate mirror reflects the image of Alice, her eldest daughter.*
FACING PAGE: *Carla's bedroom has an arched ceiling decorated with flower motifs. The head board is made from a piece of 18th-century carved panelling.*

LINKS: *Im Schlafzimmer von Carla zeigt ein verschnörkelter Spiegel das Abbild der ältesten Tochter Alice.*
RECHTE SEITE: *Die gewölbte Decke in Carlas Schlafzimmer ist mit floralen Motiven verziert. Das hölzerne Kopfende des Bettes stammt aus dem 18. Jahrhundert.*

A GAUCHE: *Dans la chambre à coucher de Carla, un miroir tarabiscoté renvoie l'image d'Alice, sa fille aînée.*
PAGE DE DROITE: *La chambre de Carla possède un plafond voûté à décorations florales. La tête du lit est un élément de boiserie 18ᵉ.*

RIGHT: *In the same room, one corner is occupied by a 19th-century baroque mirror, a Forties' lamp and several pairs of thoroughly modern shoes.*

RECHTS: *Im selben Raum befinden sich ein »barocker« Spiegel aus dem 19. Jahrhundert, eine Lampe mit einem Vierzigerjahre-Schirm und einige schicke Schuhe, die in eine Ecke verbannt wurden.*

A DROITE: *Dans la même pièce, un miroir baroque 19ᵉ, une lampe à abat-jour des années 1940 et quelques paires de chaussures très actuelles ont été relégués dans un coin.*

ZUPPA DI PANE | RIBOLLITA

Take 500 g of fresh white beans and boil them for 30 minutes. Fry together chopped carrots, a few sprigs of parsley and three or four chopped red onions in four tablespoons of good olive oil. Then add one finely chopped Swiss chard and one finely chopped Savoy cabbage. Add the beans, cover and simmer this mixture for two hours. About half way through the cooking, add four cups of beef stock with the fat removed, a few slices of bacon – try to find ham fat with the skin still intact – and 200 g of old cheese rinds (!). When the cooking is done, take a large cast-iron casserole and cover the bottom with slices of stale bread. Cover the bread with alternate layers of thick soup and bread until the casserole is filled to the brim. Put on the lid and cook over a low flame for a further two hours. The resultant heavy soup is known as "zuppa di pane", but if you reheat it the following day it becomes "ribollita", or reboiled soup.

Kochen Sie ein halbes Kilo frische weiße Bohnen eine halbe Stunde. Dünsten Sie in Scheiben geschnittene Karotten, einige Stängel Petersilie und drei bis vier rote Zwiebeln in einigen Löffeln extra-nativem Olivenöl und fügen Sie einen fein gehackten Mangold und einen fein gehackten Kopf Wirsing hinzu. Geben Sie die Bohnen dazu, und lassen Sie alles bei geschlossenem Deckel zwei Stunden köcheln. Nach der Hälfte der Kochzeit ungefähr vier Tassen magere Rinderbrühe hinzufügen, außerdem einige Scheiben Speck – nehmen Sie nach Möglichkeit Schinkenspeck mit Haut – und 200 Gramm alte Käserinde (!). Nach dem Ende der Kochzeit nehmen Sie einen großen Schmortopf und bedecken den Topfboden mit altbackenen Weißbrotscheiben. Verteilen Sie auf dem Brot die gleiche Menge der Suppe und schichten Sie nach diesem Prinzip abwechselnd Brot und Suppe auf. Wenn der Topf gut gefüllt ist, bei geschlossenem Deckel zwei Stunden köcheln lassen. Diese Spezialität heißt »zuppa di pane«, aber noch einmal aufgewärmt wird sie zu »ribollita«!

Prenez une livre de haricots blancs frais et laissez-les cuire pendant une demi-heure. Faites revenir des carottes coupées en rondelles, quelques branches de persil, trois à quatre oignons rouges dans quelques cuillerées d'huile d'olive extra vierge et ajoutez un chou noir et des choux verts finement hachés. Ajoutez les haricots, couvrez et laissez mijoter pendant deux heures. Vers la mi-cuisson, ajoutez quatre tasses de bouillon de bœuf dégraissé, quelques tranches de lard – essayez d'obtenir du jambonneau avec sa peau ! – et 200 grammes de croûtes (!) d'un vieux fromage. Quand la cuisson est terminée, prenez une très grande casserole en fonte et couvrez le fond de ce récipient avec des tranches de pain rassis. Couvrez le pain d'une quantité égale de la grosse « soupe » que vous venez d'obtenir et continuez ainsi: une couche de pain, une couche de soupe, une couche de pain etc. Quand la casserole est bien remplie, couvrez et laissez mijoter pendant deux heures. Le gros potage obtenu s'appelle « zuppa di pane », mais une fois réchauffé le lendemain, il devient une « ribollita » ou « plat réchauffé » !

The remains of a simple, delicious Tuscan lunch. The table is set in the adjoining small courtyard, a "fin-de-siècle" grotto.

Das Mittagessen im angrenzenden kleinen Innenhof, einer »Fin-de-siècle«-Grotte, ist beendet. Zurück bleiben die Reste einer ebenso köstlichen wie einfachen toskanischen Mahlzeit.

Le déjeuner dans la courette annexe, une « grotte fin de siècle », vient de s'achever. Restent les vestiges d'un repas simple et délicieux dont les Toscans ont le secret!

PODERE SCOPETO DEI CAVALLI

Beatrice Cazac

Montalcino

Beatrice Cazac remembers – perhaps with a twinge of regret – the time when Montalcino and its surrounding country was not yet besieged by tourists. It is hard to believe that she is only talking about the Seventies. Since then the birthplace of the great Brunello wine has witnessed the arrival of a modern tide of visitors, attracted by its history and its great wines. Nevertheless Beatrice can be proud that it was she and nobody else who found Scopeto dei Cavalli, for this farm – whose oldest part dates from the 16th century – lies hidden in a remote corner of the Montalcinese district, tucked away on a steep wooded hillside. Enlisting the help of the Cooper brothers, Englishmen who specialise in the restoration of old houses, Beatrice – who also is English – stipulated that there should be no interference with the basic authenticity of Scopeto dei Cavalli (literally, Horses' Wood). Apart from the conversion of the stables into a comfortable sitting room and the installation of a bathroom, the house has retained every bit of its originality and charm. Surrounded by her family, her many friends, dogs, chickens, goats, olive trees and vines, Beatrice revels in the luxury of life at one remove from the rest of the world, far from the din of the masses and the looming menace of the 21st century.

LEFT: *a horseshoe nailed to the door for good luck.*
ABOVE: *At Scopeto dei Cavalli, spring water flavoured with lemon juice is a favourite refreshment.*

LINKS: *Das Hufeisen über der Tür soll Glück bringen.*
OBEN: *Auf Scopeto dei Cavalli hilft Quellwasser mit einem Spitzer Zitronensaft gegen den Durst.*

A GAUCHE: *Le fer à cheval cloué sur une porte est censé porter bonheur.*
CI-DESSUS: *Au Scopeto, on se désaltère avec de l'eau de source citronnée.*

Beatrice Cazac erinnert sich noch gut und etwas bedauernd an die Zeit, als Montalcino und Umgebung noch nicht von Touristen heimgesucht wurde; und auch wenn man es kaum glauben mag, sie spricht dabei über die Siebzigerjahre. Seitdem hat das Geburtsland des berühmten Brunello unzählige Menschen angelockt, und so ist Beatrice zu Recht stolz darauf, den Bauernhof Scopeto dei Cavalli entdeckt zu haben. Denn dieser Hof, dessen ältester Teil aus dem 16. Jahrhundert stammt, liegt gut versteckt in einem abgelegenen Winkel der Region am steilen Abhang eines bewaldeten Hügels. Mit Hilfe ihrer englischen Landsleute, der Brüder Cooper, die sich auf die Restaurierung alter Gebäude spezialisiert haben, ist es Beatrice gelungen, die authentische Atmosphäre ihres Anwesens zu erhalten, dessen Name »Pferdewäldchen« bedeutet. Abgesehen von den Pferdeställen, die in einen behaglichen Wohnraum verwandelt wurden, und von dem neu installierten Bad wurde an dem Haus nichts verändert, sodass es immer noch seinen ursprünglichen Charme ausstrahlt. Umgeben von ihrer Familie, den zahlreichen Freunden, Hunden, Hühnern, Ziegen, Olivenhainen und Weinbergen kann sich Beatrice den Luxus erlauben, fernab vom Lärm und Trubel des 21. Jahrhunderts zu leben.

Il Scopeto dei Cavalli and the steep, narrow lane leading to Montalcino.

Scopeto dei Cavalli und der schmale steile Weg, der nach Montalcino führt.

Scopeto dei Cavalli et le petit chemin étroit et raide qui mène à Montalcino.

Beatrice Cazac se souvient – avec un soupçon de regret – du temps où Montalcino et ses alentours n'étaient pas encore assiégés par les touristes. Même si on a du mal à le croire, il ne s'agit pas d'une époque si lointaine, puisqu'elle évoque les années 1970. Depuis, le pays natal du célèbre Brunello a vu affluer les masses curieuses de son histoire et avides de goûter son grand vin. Beatrice, quant à elle, est fort satisfaite d'y avoir déniché Scopeto dei Cavalli, une ferme dont la plus ancienne partie date du 16e siècle. En effet, dissimulée dans un coin perdu de la campagne montalcinaise, la demeure se dérobe aux regards des curieux en se cramponnant au flanc en pente raide d'une colline boisée. Aidée par les frères Cooper, des Anglais spécialisés dans la restauration de demeures anciennes, Beatrice s'est démenée avec ses compatriotes pour ne pas toucher à l'authenticité de sa « broussaille des chevaux ». Sa peine a été récompensée: mis à part la transformation des écuries en séjour confortable et l'installation d'une salle de bains, la maison a gardé toute son originalité et tout son charme. Entourée par sa famille, ses nombreux amis, ses chiens, ses poules, ses chèvres, ses oliviers et ses vignes, Beatrice peut s'offrir le luxe de vivre à l'écart du monde, loin des bruits de la foule et de la menace du 21e siècle.

Beatrice has created a small terrace in front of the house – using an old kitchen table and a few benches.

Vor dem Haus hat Beatrice eine schlichte Terrasse angelegt und mit einem alten Küchentisch und einigen Bänken ausgestattet.

Devant la maison, Beatrice a créé une terrasse modeste à l'aide d'une vieille table de cuisine et de quelques bancs.

LEFT: *The walls and beams in Beatrice's bedroom are all whitewashed, and there's a ravishing view across the green valley from her balcony.*
FACING PAGE: *Farfalla the Dalmatian, fast asleep in an armchair by the heavy old fireplace.*

LINKS: *Die Wände und Deckenbalken im Zimmer von Beatrice sind weiß gekalkt. Vom Balkon aus hat sie einen herrlich weiten Blick in das grüne Tal.*
RECHTE SEITE: *Farfalla, der Dalmatiner, ist in einem Sessel vor dem alten Kamin eingenickt …*

A GAUCHE: *Les murs et les poutres de la chambre de Beatrice ont été blanchis à la chaux et, de son balcon, elle a une vue ravissante sur le vallon.*
PAGE DE DROITE: *Farfalla, le dalmatien s'est endormi dans un fauteuil devant la vielle cheminée imposante.*

PREVIOUS PAGES: *During the heat of the day, all the curtains are drawn and one of the dogs has taken refuge in the shade.*
RIGHT: *You don't need much to make a pleasant bathroom – just a half-timbered wall, an old basin and a bead curtain.*

VORHERGEHENDE DOPPELSEITE: *Es ist heiß, sämtliche Vorhänge sind geschlossen, und einer der Hunde hat sich in den Schatten zurückgezogen.*

RECHTS: *Man benötigt nicht viel für ein einladendes Badezimmer: Eine Ziegelsteinmauer, ein schlichtes altes Waschbecken und ein Holzperlenvorhang genügen …*

DOUBLE PAGE PRÉCÉDENTE: *Il fait très chaud, les rideaux sont tirés et un des chiens a cherché refuge à l'ombre.*

A DROITE: *Il faut si peu pour faire une agréable salle de bains: un mur à colombages, un ancien lavabo et un rideau à franges de bambou …*

TENUTA DI TRINORO

Andrea Franchetti

Sarteano

To attempt a description of the beauty of Tenuta di Trinoro in a few lines borders on sacrilege, because it is almost impossible to capture its splendours in words. About twenty-five years ago Andrea Franchetti immersed himself body and soul in a project which seemed perfectly mad at the time. The idea was to transform 2 000 hectares of arid land in the Orcia valley, south of Siena, into an internationally recognised vineyard. To say that he has succeeded would be an understatement; with matchless tenacity, courage and the unrestrained deployment of bulldozers this tall, fairheaded winegrower has managed to make Tenuta di Trinoro wine the uncontested number one of its kind. At the same time, Franchetti was determined to make his own permanent home in this lovely corner of Tuscany, and accordingly installed himself in a fortified 11th-century tower on the estate. The interiors of Franchetti's house are remarkable for their beauty and austerity, all decorated in a minimalistic style that borders on the ascetic. The eye lingers pleasurably on venerable painted wardrobes, sturdy tables, rustic chairs, uneven tiled floors and rough walls with no pictures to distract the eye. Andrea Franchetti pours out a glass of his delicious wine, a ray of sunshine lingers on a bowl piled high with ripe tomatoes, and "la vita è bella" …

A bouquet of herbs, wilting in a terracotta jug.

Ein Kräuterstrauß in einem Terrakottakrug dürstet nach Wasser.

Un bouquet de fines herbes assoiffées languit dans une cruche en terre cuite.

Die Tenuta di Trinoro ist im wahrsten Sinne des Wortes unbeschreiblich schön, und es erscheint fast unmöglich, diese Schönheit in einige wenige Worte zu fassen – die Fotos müssen das ihrige dazu beitragen. Es war vor beinahe 25 Jahren, als sich Andrea Franchetti mit Leib und Seele in ein Vorhaben stürzte, das völlig unmöglich schien: Er wollte 2 000 Hektar trockenes Land im Orcia-Tal südlich von Siena in ein Weinbaugebiet von internationalem Rang verwandeln. Dieses Ziel hat er tatsächlich mehr als erreicht. Mit viel Hartnäckigkeit, persönlichem Engagement und dem Einsatz einiger Bulldozer stampfte der groß gewachsene, blonde Weinbauer Tenuta di Trinoro aus dem Boden und machte aus seinem Wein ein unbestrittenes Spitzenprodukt. Und da Andrea auch im hügeligen Herzen dieses paoradiesischen Fleckens der Toskana leben wollte, richtete er sich in einem ehemaligen Befestigungsturm aus dem 11. Jahrhundert ein. Die Innenräume des Palazzo sind von bemerkenswerter Schlichtheit und Schönheit. In der Küche, dem Wohnzimmer, Bad und den Schlafzimmern regiert eine fast asketische Kargheit. Das Auge des Betrachters wandert genüsslich von den alten Schränken über die massiven Tische und Bauernstühle, den unregelmäßigen Boden aus Terrakottafliesen zu den unebenen Wänden, an denen kein Gemälde den Blick ablenkt. Andrea Franchetti bietet uns ein Glas seines delikaten Weins an, ein Sonnenstrahl fällt auf eine mit »pomodori« gefüllte Schale, und »la vita è bella« …

The entrance is crowned by a dome of cyclamen-coloured stone reminiscent of Byzantine architecture.

Der Eingang wird von einer zyklamfarbenen Steinkuppel überwölbt, eine Hommage an die byzantinische Architektur.

L'entrée est coiffée d'un dôme en pierre couleur cyclamen, réminiscence de l'architecture byzantine.

Décrire la beauté de la Tenuta di Trinoro en quelques lignes frise l'irrévérence car il est impossible de rendre ainsi vraiment la splendeur des lieux. Il y a près d'un quart de siècle que Franchetti s'est jeté corps et âme sur un projet qui semblait une folie manifeste: transformer 2 000 hectares de terre arides dans la vallée d'Orcia au sud de Sienne en un domaine viticole de renommée internationale. Dire qu'il a réussi le pari est une expression trop modérée: à coup de courage et de bulldozers, ce grand blond obstiné a fait de la Tenuta di Trinoro et de son vin un « numero uno » incontesté. Et comme il voulait vivre au cœur de ce coin de paradis toscan vallonné, il s'est installé dans une tour fortifiée du 11e siècle. Les intérieurs du palazzo sont d'une beauté et d'une sobriété remarquables, et dans la cuisine, le séjour, la salle de bains et les chambres à coucher règne un dépouillement qui frôle l'ascétisme. L'œil s'attarde avec plaisir sur des armoires anciennes à la peinture écaillée, sur des tables robustes et des chaises campagnardes, des sols irréguliers en «cotto» et des murs rugueux où aucun tableau ne vient distraire le regard. Andrea Franchetti nous sert un verre de son délicieux grand vin, un rayon de soleil s'attarde sur une jatte remplie de « pomodori » gorgées de soleil, et « la vita è bella » …

The house looks out from its hilltop across the vineyards of Tenuta di Trinoro.

Der Palazzo auf der Anhöhe überragt die Weinberge der Tenuta di Trinoro.

Du haut de sa colline, le palazzo domine les vignobles de la Tenuta di Trinoro.

Ochre walls, a "cotto"
floor and rustic furni-
ture ... all the charm
of rural Tuscany is
reflected in the deco-
ration of the kitchen.

Ockerfarbene Wände,
ein Boden aus Terra-
kottafliesen und
Bauernmöbel! Der
ganze Charme der
ländlichen Toskana
spiegelt sich in der
Dekoration der Küche.

Des murs ocre, un sol
en terre cuite et des
meubles campagnards!
Tout le charme de la
Toscane rurale se reflète
dans la décoration de
la cuisine.

LEFT: *A "prosciutto" ham, from which the first slices have just been taken, sits on top of a barrel.*
FOLLOWING PAGES: *A bright red coat hanging from the top of a linen cupboard echoes the colour of the tomato-filled jars lined up on the shelves of an 18th-century cobalt-blue dresser.*

LINKS: *Auf dem alten Fass bietet der angeschnittene »prosciutto« einen appetitlichen Anblick.*
FOLGENDE DOPPELSEITE: *Der rote Mantel am Wäscheschrank findet farblich ein Echo in den »pomodori«-Gläsern, die in den Regalen eines kobaltblauen Schrankes aus dem 18. Jahrhundert aufgereiht sind.*

A GAUCHE: *Sur un vieux tonneau, un jambon entamé forme un petit tableau appétissant.*
DOUBLE PAGE SUIVANTE: *Un manteau rouge vif accroché au rebord d'une armoire à linge fait écho aux bocaux remplis de « pomodori » alignés sur les rangements d'un meuble 18ᵉ peint en bleu cobalt.*

FACING PAGE: *Andrea Franchetti is a real gourmet – a "buongustaio" – and the sideboard of his kitchen is full of spices, dry pasta, olive oils and vinegars of all kinds.*
RIGHT: *A few dozen ripe tomatoes have been left in the shady hallway out of the oppressive heat.*

LINKE SEITE: *Andrea Franchetti ist ein echter Gourmet, ein »buongustaio« – und auf der Anrichte in seiner Küche finden sich Kräuter, Pasta, Olivenöl und mehrere Essigsorten.*
RECHTS: *In der schattigen Kühle des Eingangsbereiches lagern einige Dutzend »pomodori«.*

PAGE DE GAUCHE: *Andrea Franchetti est un vrai gourmet – un « buongustaio » – et le buffet de sa cuisine est rempli d'épices, de pâtes, d'huile d'olive et de vinaigres.*
A DROITE: *Dans la fraîcheur ombragée de l'entrée, quelques douzaines de tomates reposent à l'abri de la chaleur accablante.*

ABOVE: *In one of the bedrooms, the sobriety of the decor exactly offsets the austere architecture of the house. The Empire bed is made of mahogany.*

RIGHT: *The light in the linen room has a similar quality to the "chiaroscuro" of the Renaissance masters.*

FACING PAGE: *In a guest bedroom, the head of the 19th-century bed is decorated with flower motifs.*

OBEN: *In einem der Schlafzimmer betont die karge Einrichtung die nüchterne Architektur des Palazzo. Das Empire-Bett ist aus Mahagoni.*

RECHTS: *Das Spiel von Licht und Schatten in der Wäschekammer erinnert an das »chiaroscuro«, das Helldunkel, eines typischen Renaissance-Gemäldes.*

RECHTE SEITE: *Blumenmotive zieren das Kopfende des Betts aus dem 19. Jahrhundert in einem der Gästezimmer.*

CI-DESSUS: *Dans une des chambres, la sobriété du décor va de pair avec l'architecture dépouillée. Le lit Empire est en acajou.*

A DROITE: *Le clair-obscur qui règne dans la lingerie évoque les tableaux des maîtres de la Renaissance.*

PAGE DE DROITE: *Dans une chambre d'amis, la tête du lit 19e est décorée de motifs floraux.*

VITTORIA E ENZO GRIFONI

Chiusi

Twenty years ago the young Roman interior designer Cesare Rovatti was called to the bedside of a Tuscan country house like a doctor to a patient whose life hung in the balance. The place was hardly a ruin; on the contrary, it was a beautiful stone building in excellent repair. But its owners, Vittoria and Enzo Grifoni, had a feeling that Cesare might find a way to tame their cavernous old pile and bestow upon it the atmosphere of an English country house. And so it proved. Rovatti was able to get the best out of the vaulted, typically "chiaroscuro" rooms. His range of delicate pale ochres, golden browns, grey-greens, straw yellows and a subtle variety of bronzes blended perfectly with the rustic Italian furniture dating from the 18th and 19th centuries. The style also went well with the Grifonis' assortment of Victoriana – tapestry-covered cushions, bronze animals, oddly realistic earthenware bulldogs and a multitude of English paintings representing animals of every shape and size. The owners, who come to Chiusi to escape their hyperactive professional lives in Rome, still go into ecstasies over the view across their English park from their bedroom balcony. Within is a pretty four-poster bed – and a space in which Rovatti has yet again proved that classical interiors never go out of fashion and that his decor is still as fresh and young as ever.

Beware of the dog!

Achtung Wachhund!

Attention, le chien monte la garde!

The house is surrounded by a beautiful English-style park.

Das Haus umgibt ein schöner englischer Park.

La maison est entourée d'un très beau parc à l'anglaise.

Vor zwanzig Jahren wurde der junge Innenarchitekt Cesare Rovatti aus Rom mit einer solchen Dringlichkeit in ein Landhaus in der Toskana bestellt, wie man sonst einen Notarzt ans Krankenbett ruft! Die Besitzer Vittoria und Enzo Grifoni hatten sich in den Kopf gesetzt, dass Cesare dem weitläufigen Anwesen das Flair eines »English Country House« verleihen könnte. Tatsächlich gelang es Rovatti, die Vorzüge der großen Räume hervorzuheben, in denen Licht und Schatten miteinander spielen. Seine Palette zeigt helles Ocker, Goldbraun, Graugrün, Strohgelb und mehrere Bronzeschattierungen. Diese Farbtöne harmonieren gut mit den antiken italienischen Möbeln und den viktorianischen Sammelstücken der Grifonis: Kissen mit Teppichbezug, Bronzetiere, eine verblüffend lebendig wirkende Keramik-Bulldogge und zahlreiche englische Gemälde mit Tieren aller Größen und Arten. Die Eigentümer erholen sich hier am Wochenende von ihrem Berufsalltag in Rom. Immer wieder begeistern sie sich für die Aussicht auf den englischen Park, wenn sie auf der Terrasse ihres Schlafzimmers stehen. Hier hat Rovatti erneut bewiesen, dass klassische Interieurs nie aus der Mode kommen: Seine Ausstattung wirkt immer noch zeitlos schön.

Il y a 20 ans, le jeune décorateur romain Cesare Rovatti fut appelé au chevet d'une maison de campagne toscane comme un médecin que l'on appelle d'urgence au chevet d'un grand malade! La belle demeure en pierre rustique n'était pas une ruine, au contraire. Mais ses propriétaires Enzo et Vittoria Grifoni pensaient que Cesare pourrait maîtriser les volumes de cette grande bâtisse et lui donner ce côté « manoir anglais » qui leur tenait à cœur. Rovatti a su tirer le meilleur parti de ces grandes pièces voûtées où jouent l'ombre et la lumière, et sa palette aux tons délicats – des ocres clairs, des bruns dorés, des vert-de-gris, des jaunes paille et des nuances de bronze – se marie à merveille avec les meubles rustiques italiens du 18e et du 19e siècles et avec cette collection hétéroclite nommée Victoriana composée de coussins en tapisserie, d'animaux en bronze, de bouledogues en faïence et d'une multitude de tableaux anglais représentant toutes sortes d'animaux. Les propriétaires qui se reposent ici de leur vie professionnelle trop active à Rome s'extasient toujours à la vue du parc à l'anglaise depuis la terrasse de la chambre à coucher. Une chambre où trône un joli lit à baldaquin et où Rovatti, une fois de plus, nous prouve que les intérieurs classiques ne se démodent jamais et que sa décoration, âgée d'un quart de siècle, n'a pas pris une seule ride.

Light and shadow dapple a window which is already enhanced by a box of geraniums.

Licht- und Schattenspiele auf einem Fenster mit einem Geranienkasten.

La lumière danse sur une fenêtre embellie par une jardinière garnie de géraniums.

The spacious, beautiful
kitchen is notable for
its tiles, which cover the
floor, walls and fire-
place, and for its rustic
pine furniture.

Das Besondere an dieser
schönen großen Küche
sind die hellen Holz-
möbel und die Fliesen
an Boden, Wänden und
Kamin.

Belle et vaste, la cuisine
se distingue par son
décor à carrelages qui
couvre le sol, les murs et
la cheminée rustique et
par son mobilier cam-
pagnard en bois blond.

LEFT: *The spirit of the 19th century predominates in this romantic guest bedroom: moss-green walls, wrought-iron bedsteads and oil lamps.*
FACING PAGE: *The key of this painted wooden wardrobe is hung with a passementerie tassel.*

LINKS: *Der Geist des 19. Jahrhunderts wird in diesem Gästezimmer mit den moosgrünen Wänden, dem schmiedeeisernen Bett und den Petroleumlampen spürbar.*
RECHTE SEITE: *An dem Schlüssel zu dem bemalten Holzschrank hängt eine Troddel.*

A GAUCHE: *L'esprit 19ᵉ règne dans cette chambre d'amis aux murs vert mousse où les lits en fer forgé et les lampes à pétrole évoquent des images teintées de romantisme.*
PAGE DE DROITE: *La clef de cette armoire en bois peint est ornée d'un gland en passementerie.*

✨Una CASA DI CAMPAGNA

Maremma

The work of Stefano Mantovani and Manuel Jiménez is studiously elegant. At the same time, when they undertake the decoration of a house, they make quite sure that the marriage between aesthetics and comfort remains a happy one. In this case the country house which awaited the attentions of Stefano and his partner had begun as a modest 18th-century construction, was then enriched over the years by the addition of a magnificent garden created by the architect Peironne, a few rooms of pleasing size and a spacious stable block. The present owners, who are from Sicily, have a passion for horses; in addition to their equestrian hobby, their daily life seems to be ruled by a love of hospitality, good cooking and the sheer delight of living in a green and beautiful landscape. Mantovani and Jiménez have achieved a "tour de force" here. They installed a new staircase, whose mezzanine with its chestnut balustrade reveals their insistence on first-class materials and a perfect finish. They also created an intimate dining room with light blue panelling, a loggia in the purest Mediterranean style and a bedroom with a pair of iron Sicilian bedsteads and walls upholstered with blue-and-white mattress ticking. In a word, this is a real family house with a warm and welcoming atmosphere.

A rearing bronze horse creates a surprising contrast with the yellow-ochre walls of the hall-way.

Das sich aufbäumende Bronzepferd bildet im Eingangsbereich einen faszinierenden Kontrast zu den ockergelben Wänden.

Un cheval cabré en bronze forme un contraste surprenant avec les murs ocre de l'entrée.

Die Kreationen des Duos Stefano Mantovani und Manuel Jiménez unterscheiden sich von denen anderer Innenarchitekten vor allem durch den Tick mehr an Eleganz. Sie verlieren nie aus den Augen, dass man Ästhetik stets mit Komfort verbinden sollte. Bei dem Landhaus, das auf die Inspiration von Stefano und seinem Partner wartete, handelte es sich um ein schlichtes Gebäude aus dem 18. Jahrhundert mit einem weitläufigen Pferdestall und einem herrlichen Garten, den der Architekt Peironne angelegt hatte. Die Hauseigentümer, die aus Sizilien stammen, sind Pferdenarren. Neben den Freuden hoch zu Ross gehören zu ihrem Alltag aber auch Gastfreundschaft, gute Küche und das Wohlgefallen, im Herzen einer grünen Landschaft zu leben. Die beiden Innenarchitekten vollbrachten für sie eine Glanzleistung. Unter anderem installierten sie ein Treppenhaus mit Absatz und Geländer aus Kastanienholz – Zeugnis ihrer Vorliebe für hochwertige Materialien und perfekte Verarbeitung. Sie entwarfen ein intimes Esszimmer mit zartblauen Vertäfelungen, eine mediterran geprägte Loggia, und für das Schlafzimmer wählten sie eine Wandbespannung aus blauweißem Matratzenstoff – kurz: ein echter Familiensitz, in dessen einladendem Ambiente es sich gut leben lässt.

Les réalisations du tandem Stefano Mantovani et Manuel Jiménez se distinguent avant tout par un grand souci de l'élégance et s'ils décident de s'occuper de la décoration d'une maison, ils ne perdent jamais de vue le mariage heureux entre l'esthétisme et le confort. La maison de campagne qui attendait le coup de baguette de Stefano et de son partenaire n'était qu'une modeste construction 18ᵉ siècle, enrichie au cours du temps d'un magnifique jardin créé par l'architecte Peironne, de quelques pièces de dimensions agréables et d'une vaste écurie. Les propriétaires, d'origine sicilienne, ont une véritable passion pour les chevaux et en dehors des plaisirs équestres, leur vie quotidienne semble gérée par l'hospitalité, la bonne cuisine et la douceur de vivre. Mantovani et Jiménez réussirent un véritable tour de force qui impliquait l'installation d'une cage d'escalier – la mezzanine et sa balustrade en châtaignier révèlent leur prédilection pour les matériaux nobles et pour une finition impeccable – et la création d'une salle à manger intime, tapissée de lambris bleu clair, d'une loggia dans le plus pur goût méditerranéen et d'une chambre à coucher tendue d'un tissu à matelas bleu et blanc et qui abrite une paire de lits en fer siciliens. En un mot: une vraie maison de famille où il fait bon vivre dans un décor accueillant et chaleureux.

FACING PAGE: *On the garden side a very old umbrella pine rises above the elongated facade of the house.*

ABOVE: *Mantovani and Jiménez constructed this imposing loggia with a view to creating an area for alfresco meals. The furniture is made of wrought iron.*

RIGHT: *The inner courtyard has an antique fountain decorated with a "mascherone".*

LINKE SEITE: *Im Garten erhebt sich eine alte Schirmpinie über die lang gestreckte Hausfassade.*

OBEN: *Mantovani und Jiménez schufen mit dieser imposanten Loggia einen malerischen Rahmen für eine Mahlzeit »al fresco«. Die Möbel sind aus Schmiedeeisen.*

RECHTS: *Den Innenhof ziert ein antikisierender Springbrunnen mit »mascherone«.*

PAGE DE GAUCHE: *Un très ancien pin parasol dresse sa sombre silhouette devant la façade oblongue de la maison.*

CI-DESSUS: *Mantovani et Jiménez ont construit cette loggia imposante afin de créer un espace pour les déjeuners et les dîners al fresco. Le mobilier est en fer forgé.*

A DROITE: *La cour intérieure se pare d'une fontaine à l'antique décorée d'un « mascherone ».*

LEFT: *For the walls of the dining room, Stefano and Manuel chose a light blue shade.*

LINKS: *Für die Wände im Esszimmer wählten Stefano und Manuel ein zartes Hellblau.*

A GAUCHE: *Stefano et Manuel ont choisi un ton bleu clair pour les murs de la salle à manger.*

FACING PAGE: *On the mantelpiece of the small dining room the mistress of the house has placed a copper flower-box filled with dried fruit.*
RIGHT: *In the entrance hall, ochre-yellow walls accentuate the bright colours of the earthen-ware and the warm tones of the furniture and fabrics.*

LINKE SEITE: *Auf dem Kaminsims im kleinen Esszimmer hat die Hausherrin einen Blumenkasten aus Kupfer mit vielen getrockneten Früchten dekoriert.*
RECHTS: *In der Ein-gangshalle betonen die ockergelben Wände die lebhaften Farben der Keramikvasen, der Möbel und Stoffe.*

PAGE DE GAUCHE: *Sur la cheminée de la petite salle à manger, la maîtresse de maison a posé une jardinière en cuivre remplie de fruits séchés.*
A DROITE: *Dans le hall d'entrée, des murs ocre mettent en valeur les couleurs vives des faïences ainsi que les tonalités chaudes du mobilier et des tissus.*

LEFT: *In the principal bedroom, the occupants sleep in polychrome wrought-iron beds which the family inherited from their Sicilian ancestors.*
FACING PAGE: *Mantovani and Jiménez upholstered the walls of this bedroom with an inexpensive blue-and-white floral fabric to emphasise the countrified aspect of the decoration. The alarm clock and the pewter thermos are period pieces.*

LINKS: *Im Schlafzimmer der Hausherrin stehen bemalte Eisenbetten, die sie von einem ihrer sizilianischen Vorfahren geerbt hat.*
RECHTE SEITE: *Mantovani und Jiménez bespannten die Wände dieses Schlafzimmers mit einem preiswerten blauweißen Blumenstoff, der das*

ländliche Flair betont. Der Wecker und die Thermoskanne aus Zinn sind alte Stücke!

A GAUCHE: *Dans la chambre maîtresse, les habitants dorment dans des lits en fer polychromes hérités d'un ancêtre sicilien.*

PAGE DE DROITE: *Mantovani et Jiménez ont tendu les murs de cette chambre d'un tissu floral bleu et blanc à deux sous pour accentuer le côté campagnard de la décoration. Le réveil-matin et le thermos en fer blanc sont d'époque !*

RIGHT: *an Art-Nouveau-style bathroom in white and blue echoes 1900 designs.*

RECHTS: *ein Badezimmer in Blau und Weiß mit all der Nostalgie von 1900.*

A DROITE: *une salle de bains Liberty bleue et blanche – nostalgie des décors 1900.*

TORRE NUOVA

San Vincenzo

Torre Nuova, an old fortified tower on the shores of the Tyr-
rhenian Sea, was constructed in the 18th century to replace an
even older building which had fallen into ruin. Thereafter it
served as a lodging for the soldiers of the garrison of the Gran
Ducato di Toscana, and was later converted into a "casa
colonica" for the use of "contadini" and their animals. The descendants of the family that bought Torre Nuova at the beginning of the 19th century – and who regularly stay there – still
remember the old farmers who once occupied the crumbling
buildings. Restored and refurnished a bare two years ago, the
"new" tower is the very image of simplicity. There are white-
washed walls and a huge salon with a great vault and robust
furniture, features which reflect the personality of the tower's
warm-hearted occupants, who are great lovers of music, the
arts and food. At Torre Nuova, life is lived with wide open
windows and doors, and diaphanous curtains which lift and
fall with the breezes. In summer the inhabitants dine on melon
and prosciutto washed down with a good local wine, and they
sleep in solid country-made beds with mosquito nets spread
over them. Outside is the intensely blue sea – blue as the sky,
and blue as the parasol stuck in the sand. How it beckons.

LEFT: *Stones found
on the beach fill a blue
earthenware goblet.*
ABOVE: *In the en-
trance, a porcelain dish
in the shape of a shell
has been placed on a
chair.*

LINKS: *Kieselsteine
vom Strand in einer
blau glasierten Schale.*
OBEN: *Im Eingangs-
bereich steht eine
muschelförmige Porzel-
lanschale auf einem
Stuhl.*

A GAUCHE: *Des galets
trouvés sur la plage dans
une coupe en faïence
bleue.*
CI-DESSUS: *Dans
l'entrée, une chaise
accueille une coquille
en porcelaine.*

Der Befestigungsturm Torre Nuova wurde im 18. Jahrhundert anstelle einer verfallenen Befestigung direkt an der Küste des Tyrrhenischen Meeres errichtet und diente den Soldaten der Garnison Gran Ducato di Toscana als Quartier. Später wurde der Turm in eine »casa colonica« – ein typisch toskanisches Bauernhaus – umgebaut, in der die »contadini«, die Bauern, und ihre Tiere Unterkunft fanden. Die Nachkommen der Familie, die Torre Nuova Anfang des 19. Jahrhunderts erwarb, kamen häufig hierher und erinnern sich noch an die alten Bauern, die zuletzt in dem verfallenen Gebäude hausten. Seit knapp zwei Jahren restauriert und neu möbliert, steht der »neue Turm« nun für schlichte Schönheit – mit weiß gekalkten Wänden und dem großzügigen Salon, den ein großer Bogen und massive Möbel zieren. Das Ambiente spiegelt die Persönlichkeit der warmherzigen Bewohner, ihre Begeisterung für Musik, Kunst und … gutes Essen! Auf Torre Nuova stehen Fenster und Türen stets weit offen, und ein leichter Luftzug bewegt die Vorhänge. Zum Essen gibt es »prosciutto e melone«, Melone mit Schinken, dazu ein Gläschen Landwein. Geschlafen wird in Bauernbetten mit Moskitonetzen. Draußen schimmert das Meer in einem intensiven Blau … so blau wie der Himmel und wie der Sonnenschirm, der, in den Sand gesteckt, zum »dolce far niente« einlädt.

Torre Nuova, une tour fortifiée à deux pas de la mer Tyrrhénienne, a été construite au 18e siècle. Elle remplaçait une tour plus ancienne tombée en ruine et devait servir de logis aux soldats de la garnison du Gran Ducato di Toscana. Plus tard, transformée en « casa colonica », elle hébergea les « contadini » et leurs animaux, et les descendants de la famille qui acheta Torre Nuova au début du 19e siècle – et qui y séjournent régulièrement – se souviennent encore des vieux fermiers qui occupaient les lieux délabrés. Restaurée et remeublée il y a deux ans à peine, la « nouvelle tour » est l'image même de la simplicité. Ses murs blanchis à la chaux et son vaste salon orné d'une grande arche et d'un mobilier robuste reflètent la personnalité de ses occupants chaleureux, grands amateurs de musique, d'art et … des plaisirs de la table ! A Torre Nuova, on vit fenêtres et portes grandes ouvertes, la brise légère soulève les rideaux diaphanes. On dîne de melon parfumé et juteux, d'une belle tranche de «prosciutto» et d'un petit vin de pays, et on dort à poings fermés dans de solides lits campagnards équipés d'une moustiquaire. Dehors, il y a la mer d'un bleu intense … Bleue comme le ciel et comme le parasol planté dans le sable et qui invite au «dolce far niente».

A private beach, a comfortable cast-iron bench and a parasol the same colour as the sea and the sky. Who could want more?

Ein Privatstrand, eine einladende gusseiserne Bank und ein Sonnenschirm, in dem sich die Farbe von Meer und Himmel wiederholen. Was braucht man mehr, um glücklich zu sein?

Une plage privée, un joli banc en fonte et un parasol couleur de mer et de ciel … en faut-il plus pour être heureux ?

LEFT: *The inhabitants preferred to retain the dilapidated look of the walls, which are covered in rough stucco.*
FACING PAGE: *Bliss in the absolute: a good book, and a good drink, beside a window that overlooks the sea.*

LINKS: *Die Bewohner haben die unregelmäßige und stellenweise angegriffene Struktur der Wände bewusst erhalten.*
RECHTE SEITE: *Der Höhepunkt der Muße: mit einem guten Buch und einem Glas Wein an einem Fenster mit Meerblick zu sitzen.*

A GAUCHE: *Les habitants ont préféré garder l'aspect délabré de ces murs couverts d'un stuc irrégulier.*
PAGE DE DROITE: *Le sommet du bien-être: un bon livre et un bon verre près d'une fenêtre qui donne sur la mer.*

RIGHT: *The coat rack beside the front door, with its burden of straw hats, makes a charming still life.*

RECHTS: *die Garderobe im Eingangsbereich mit Strohhüten und Ölzeug.*

A DROITE: *Près de la porte d'entrée, un portemanteau chargé de chapeaux de paille et de cirés forme une jolie nature morte.*

FACING PAGE: *In the former stables, where cows once lined the muddy walls, the owners have created a serenely beautiful living room.*

ABOVE: *The white-washed walls accentuate the sober feel of the rattan furniture. The contemporary painting is by a friend of the family.*

RIGHT: *Sunflowers in a niche above the sink.*

LINKE SEITE: *Im ehemaligen Stall, in dem sich früher die Kühe aneinander drängten, haben sich die Bewohner ein heiteres Wohnzimmer geschaffen.*

OBEN: *Die weiß gekalkten Wände sind der perfekte Hintergrund für die schlichten Korbmöbel und das Gemälde, das Werk einer guten Freundin.*

RECHTS: *In einer Nische über der Spüle befindet sich ein charmantes Arrangement aus Sonnenblumen.*

PAGE DE GAUCHE: *Dans l'ancienne étable, là où les vaches s'alignaient le long des murs boueux, les habitants ont créé un séjour d'une beauté sereine.*

CI-DESSUS: *Les murs blanchis à la chaux font ressortir la sobriété raffinée des meubles en rotin et d'un tableau contemporain qui porte la signature d'une amie.*

A DROITE: *Au-dessus de l'évier, une niche abrite un charmant bouquet de tournesols.*

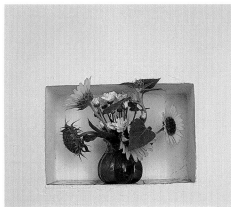

Beneath a pair of 17th-century still lifes and a wrought iron chandelier, a long refectory table and matching benches form an ideal dining area within the huge living room. Today the menu consists of mozzarella, "prosciutto" ham and ripe melons.

Unter zwei Stillleben aus dem 17. Jahrhundert und einem schmiedeeisernen Kronleuchter werden die gemeinsamen Mahlzeiten an dem langen Refektoriumstisch mit den Bänken eingenommen. Heute stehen »mozzarella« sowie »prosciutto e melone« auf dem Speiseplan!

Sous une paire de natures mortes 17e et d'un chandelier en fer forgé, une longue table de réfectoire et des bancs assortis forment un coin repas idéal dans le vaste séjour. Au menu aujourd'hui: mozzarella, jambon et melon !

LEFT: *a blue and white bathroom, cool and pleasant.*
FACING PAGE: *"Sur la plage ensoleillée" is much more than the title of a popular French ditty. At Torre Nuova, these few words express the reality of life.*

LINKS: *Wie frisch ein Badezimmer in Blau und Weiß wirkt …*
RECHTE SEITE: *»Am sonnigen Strand« lautet der Titel eines bekannten französischen Chansons. In Torre Nuova sind diese Worte Realität geworden.*

A GAUCHE: *une salle de bains bleue et blanche, une fraîcheur agréable …*
PAGE DE DROITE: *«Sur la plage ensoleillée» est bien plus que le titre d'une chanson populaire: à Torre Nuova ces quelques mots sont devenus réalité.*

RIGHT: *It is good to rest under the mosquito net, with the windows wide open, in this grand old mahogany bed.*

RECHTS: *In diesem alten Mahagonibett mit Moskitonetz lässt es sich bei offenem Fenster wunderbar schlafen.*

A DROITE: *Il fait bon dormir, fenêtres ouvertes, dans ce vieux lit en acajou sous une moustiquaire.*

ACKNOWLEDGEMENTS

DANKSAGUNG

REMERCIEMENTS

We would like to express our profound gratitude to all those who have assisted us in making this book, and especially to those people all over Tuscany who received us with such sincerity and warmth while we were doing our research. In addition to acknowledging the help of the owners and inmates of the wonderful houses shown in these pages, we wish to offer our special thanks to Mr. Giorgio Leonini, who guided us so surely in our wanderings; and to Laurie and Andrea Laschetti, Elisabetta Pandolfini, Lucia and Giuliano Civitelli, Marten van Sinderen, Roberto Budini Gattai and Valentina Buscicchio, without whom we would have been totally unable to translate the most beautiful and authentic aspects of Tuscany into words and images.

Wir möchten all jenen unsere Dankbarkeit ausdrücken, die uns bei der Realisierung dieses Buches geholfen haben. Selten sind wir so herzlich und liebenswürdig aufgenommen worden. Wir bedanken uns bei den Eigentümern und Bewohnern der herrlichen Häuser, die dieses Buch illustriert, und ganz besonders bei Giorgio Leonini, der uns ein wunderbarer Führer war, bei Laurie und Andrea Laschetti, Elisabetta Pandolfini, Lucia und Giuliano Civitelli, Marten van Sinderen, Roberto Budini Gattai und Valentina Buscicchio. Ohne sie wäre es uns nicht möglich gewesen, die Schönheit und Ursprünglichkeit der Toskana in Bilder umzusetzen.

Il est difficile de trouver les mots pour exprimer notre reconnaissance envers tous ceux qui nous ont aidés à réaliser ce livre. Nous avons rarement reçu un accueil aussi sincère et chaleureux. En dehors des propriétaires et des habitants des merveilleuses maisons qui illustrent ces pages, nous tenons à remercier vivement M. Giorgio Leonini qui fut un guide hors pair, ainsi que Laurie et Andrea Laschetti, Elisabetta Pandolfini, Lucia et Giuliano Civitelli, Marten van Sinderen, Roberto Budini Gattai et Valentina Buscicchio. Sans leur aide, il nous aurait été impossible de traduire en images ce que la Toscane possède de plus beau et de plus authentique.

Barbara & René Stoeltie

To stay informed about upcoming TASCHEN titles, please request our magazine at www.taschen.com or write to TASCHEN, Hohenzollernring 53, D-50672 Cologne, Germany, Fax: +49-221-254919. We will be happy to send you a free copy of our magazine which is filled with information about all of our books.

© 2005 TASCHEN GmbH
Hohenzollernring 53, D-50672 Köln
www.taschen.com

© 2005 VG Bild-Kunst, Bonn, for the works by Alighiero Boetti and Sol LeWitt

Design by Catinka Keul, Cologne
Layout by Angelika Taschen, Cologne
Texts edited by Ursula Fethke, Cologne
Elke Eßmann, Dortmund
Lithography by Ute Wachendorf, Cologne
English translation by Anthony Roberts, Lupiac
German translation by Marion Valentin, Cologne

Printed in Portugal

ISBN 3-8228-4247-8
(edition with English/German cover)

ISBN 3-8228-4246-X
(edition with French cover)

ENDPAPER: *Caravaggio, Basket of Fruit (c.1598/1599), Pinacoteca Ambrosiana, Milan.*
VORSATZPAPIER: *Caravaggio, Obstkorb (um 1598/1599), Pinacoteca Ambrosiana, Mailand.*
PAGES DE GARDE: *Le Caravage, Corbeille de fruits (vers 1598/1599) Pinacoteca Ambrosiana, Milan.*

PAGE 2: *A classic Tuscan bite to eat.*
SEITE 2: *Ein typisch toskanischer Imbiss.*
PAGE 2: *Une collation typiquement toscane.*

PAGE 4: *Caravaggio, Bacchus (c. 1596/1597), Detail, Galleria degli Uffizi, Florence.*
SEITE 4: *Caravaggio, Bacchus (um 1596/1597), Detail, Galleria degli Uffizi, Florenz.*
PAGE 4: *Le Caravage, Corbeille de fruits (vers 1598/1599), détail, Galleria degli Uffizi, Florence.*

PAGE 178: *Detail of Villa Vico Bello: a delicate Meissen statuette on a multicoloured 18th-century console decorated with a frivolous blue ribbon.*
SEITE 178: *Detailansicht aus der Villa Vico Bello: Eine zierliche Statue aus Meissener Porzellan thront auf der bemalten Konsole aus dem 18. Jahrhundert mit der frivolen blauen Schleife.*
PAGE 178: *Détail de la Villa Vico Bello: Une délicate statuette en porcelaine de Meissen a été placée sur une console 18e polychromée et ornée d'un frivole ruban bleu.*

TASCHEN'S
HOTEL BOOK SERIES
Edited by Angelika Taschen

"'Decorator porn', a friend calls it, those sensuous photograph books of beautiful houses. Long on details and atmosphere and packed with ideas, this is a bountiful look at beautiful but unpretentious homes in the place where 'everything is founded on the link between beauty and well-being'. It's easy to linger there."
The Virginian-Pilot, USA

IN PREPARATION:
The Hotel Book
Great Escapes North America
The Hotel Book
Great Escapes Central America
The Hotel Book
Great Escapes City

TASCHEN'S
LIVING IN SERIES
Edited by Angelika Taschen

IN PREPARATION:
Living in Bali
Living in Japan
Living in Cuba

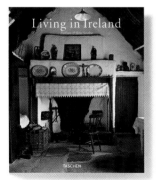

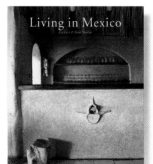

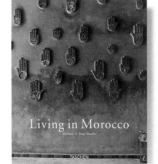

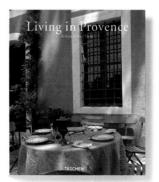